THIS BOOK BELONGS TO

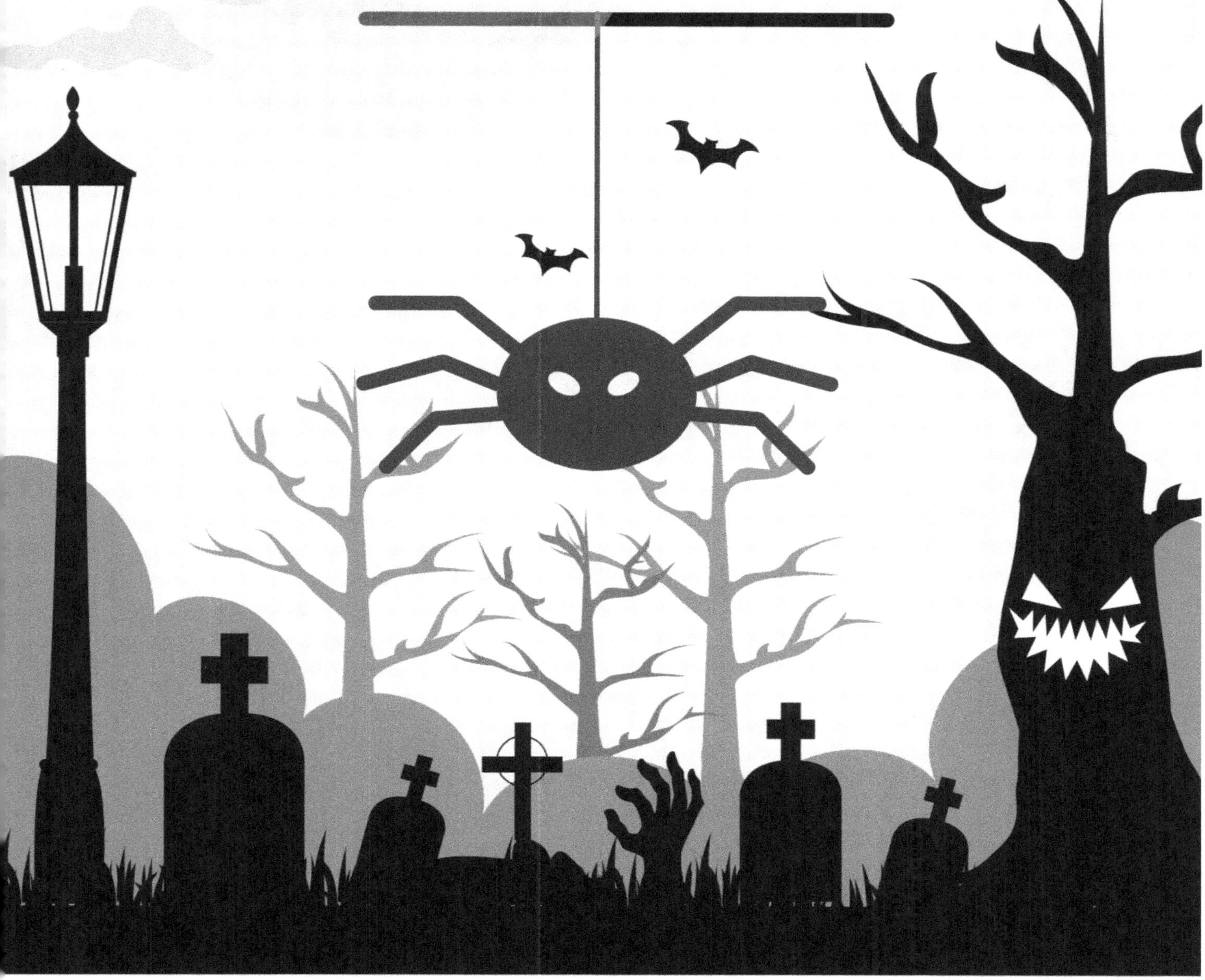

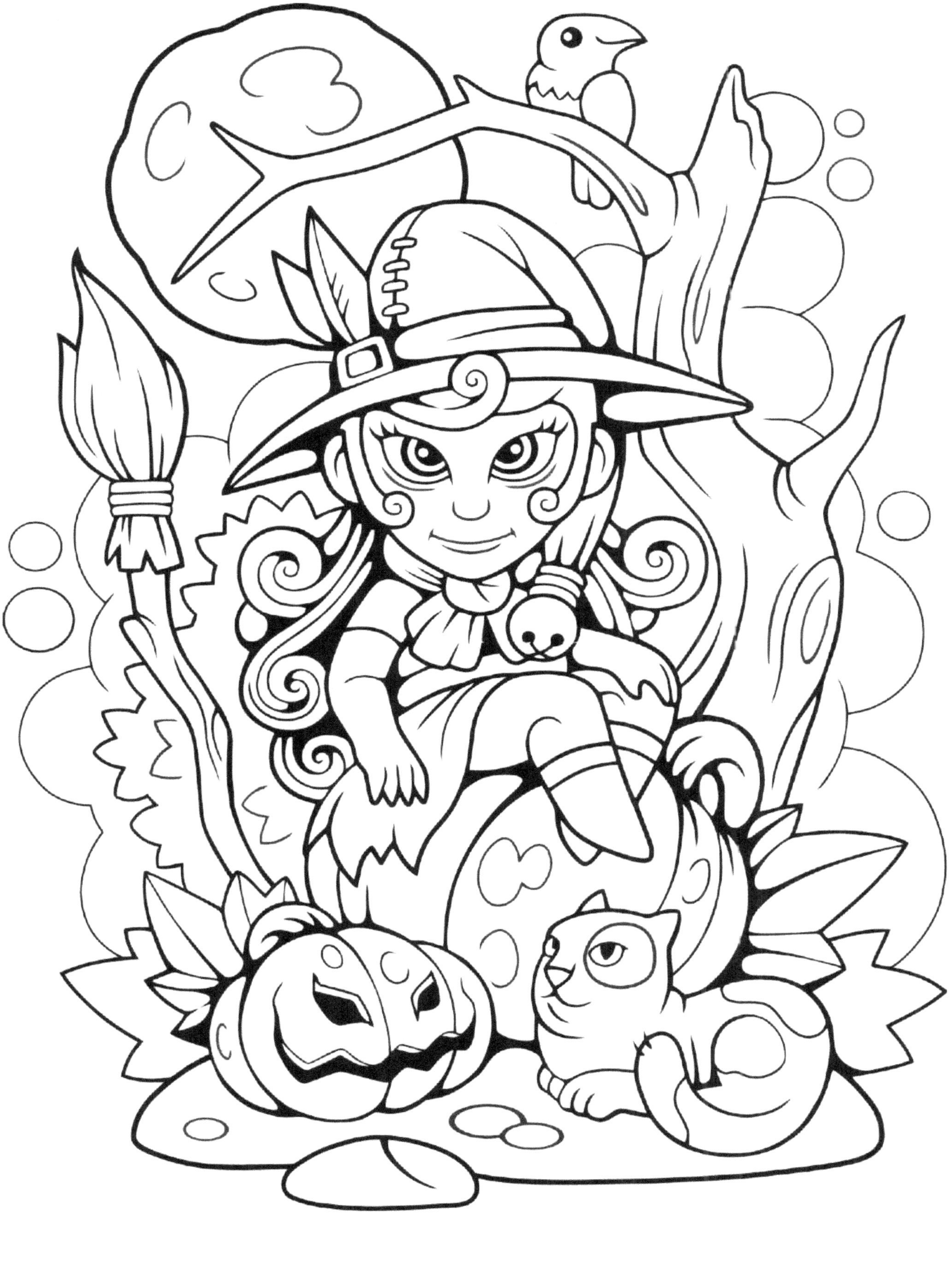

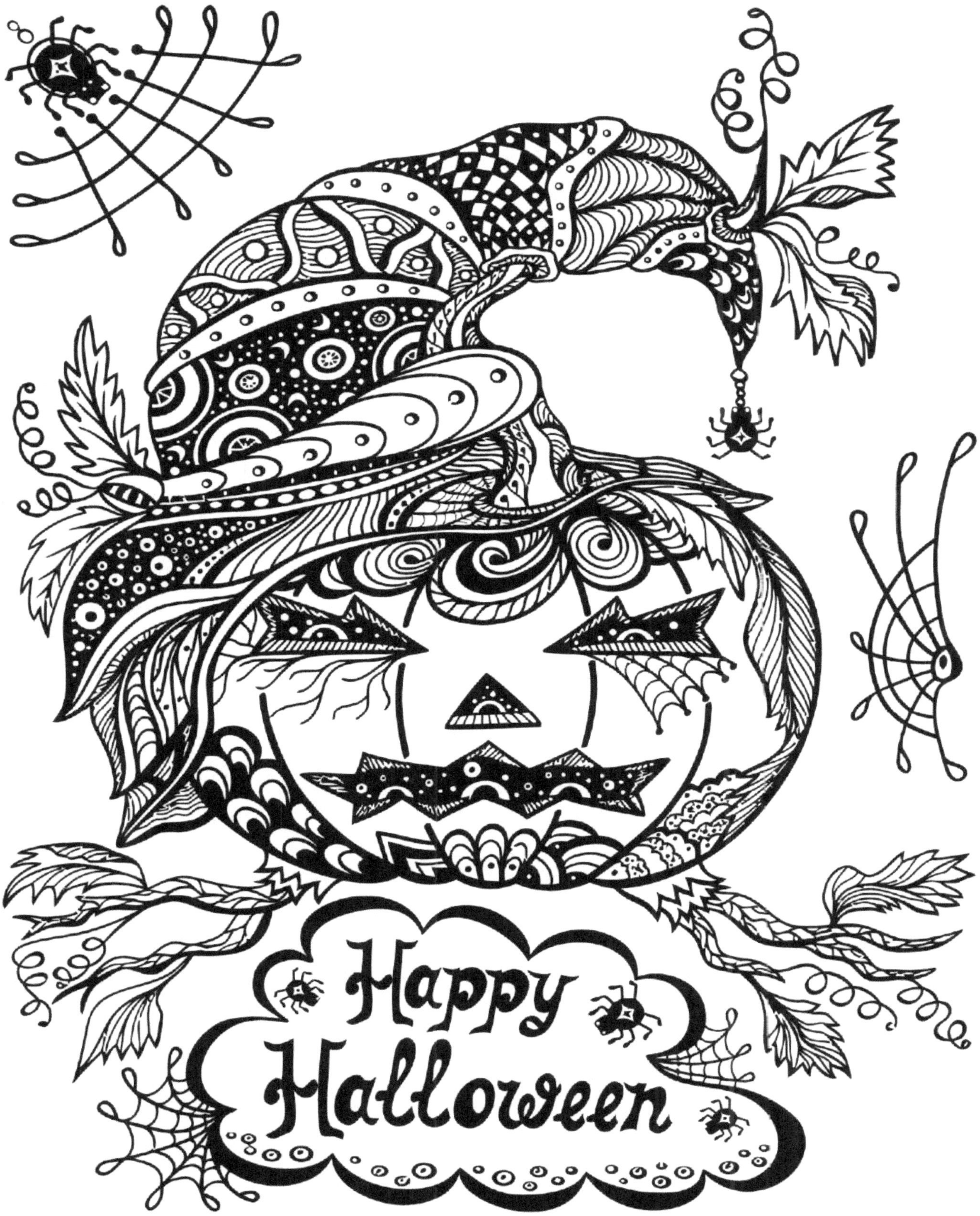
Happy
Halloween

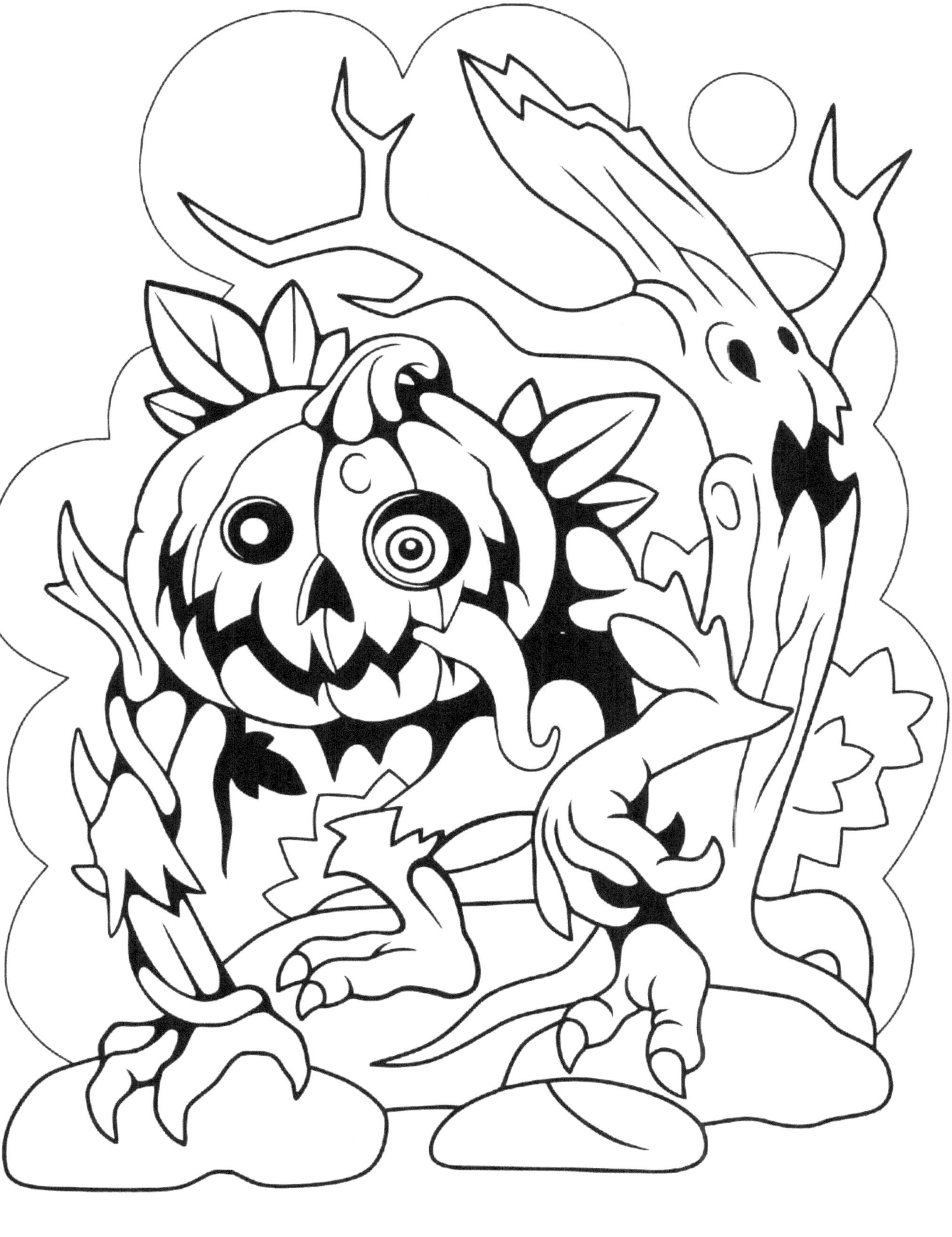

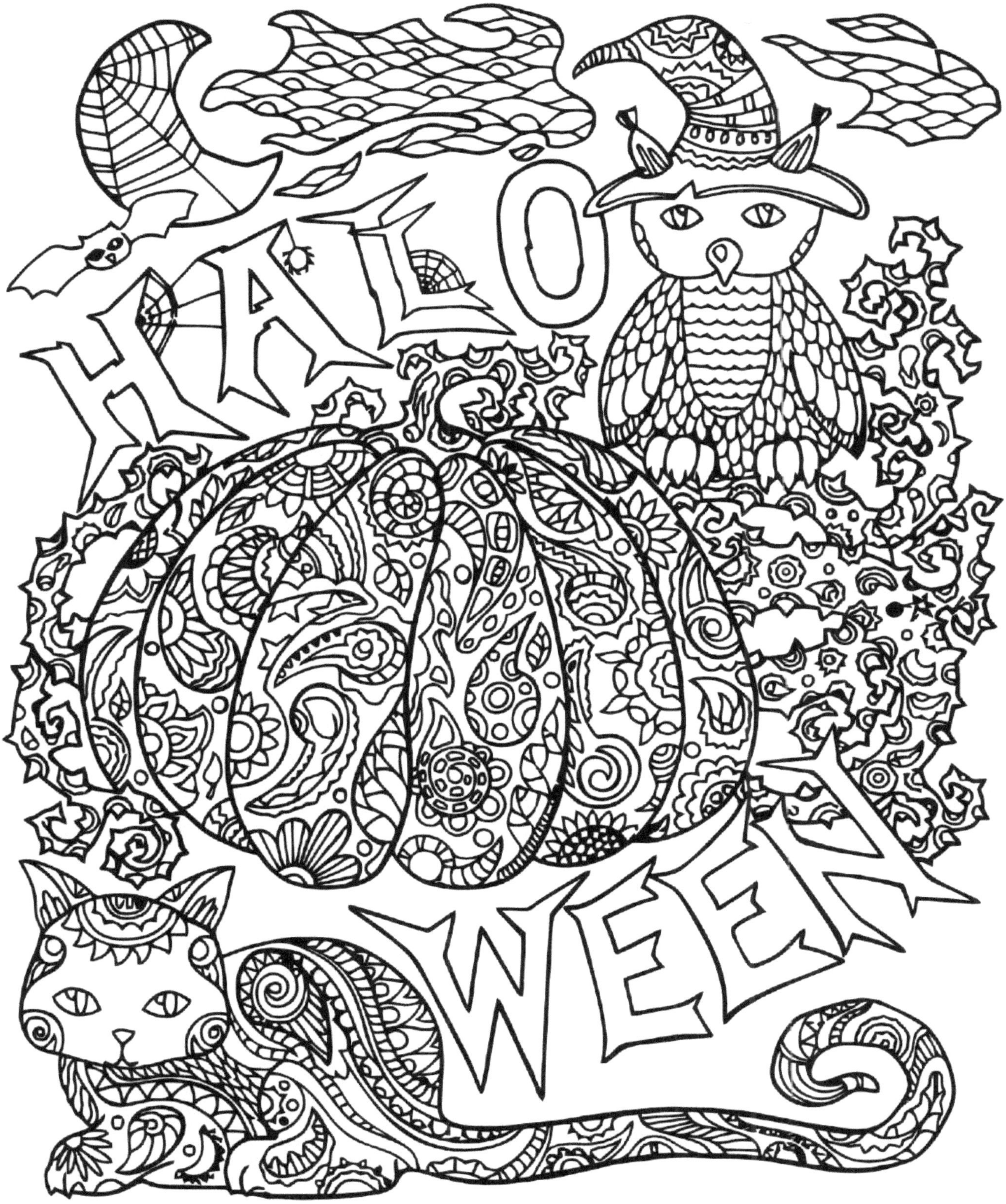
HALLO
WEEN

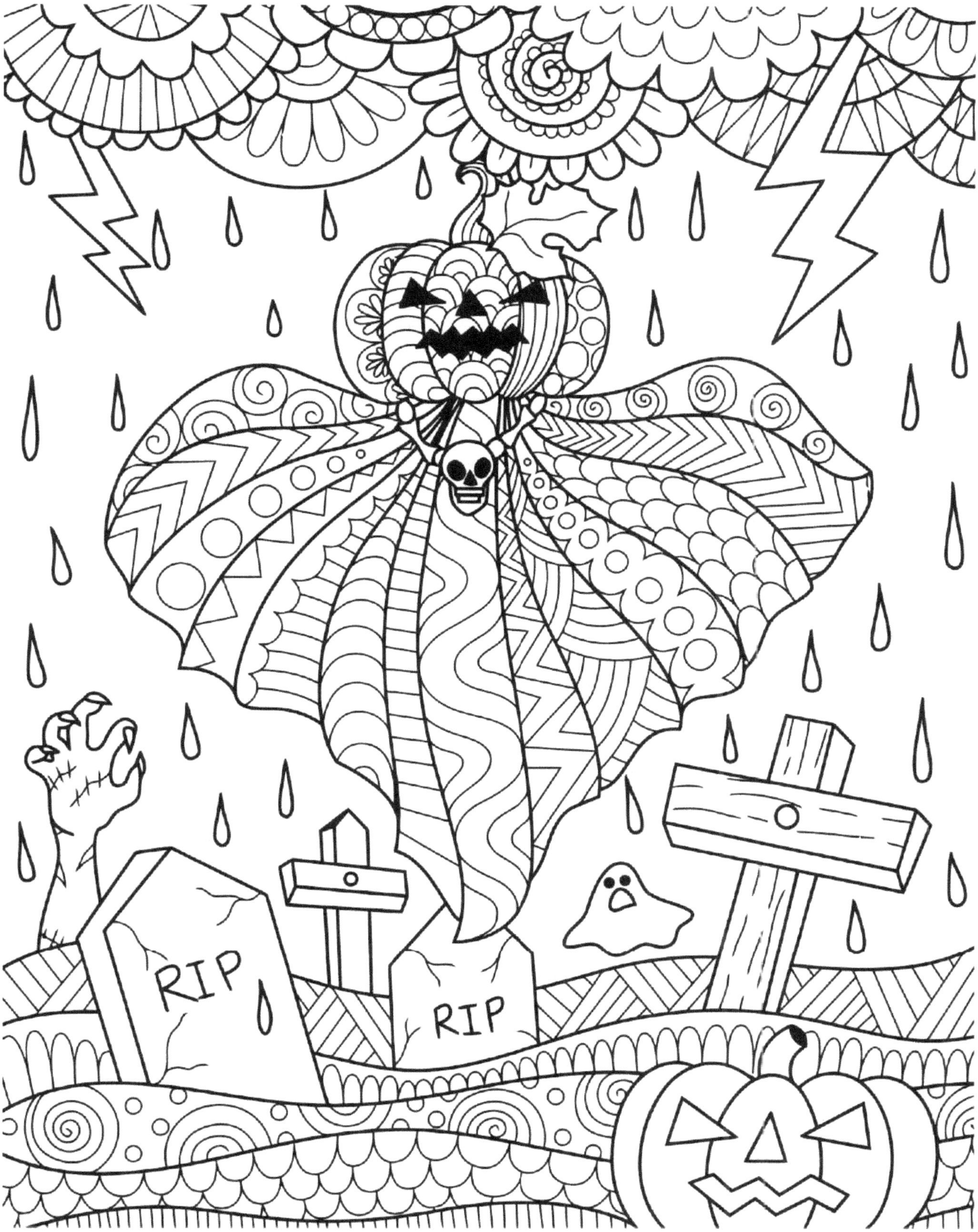
RIP
RIP

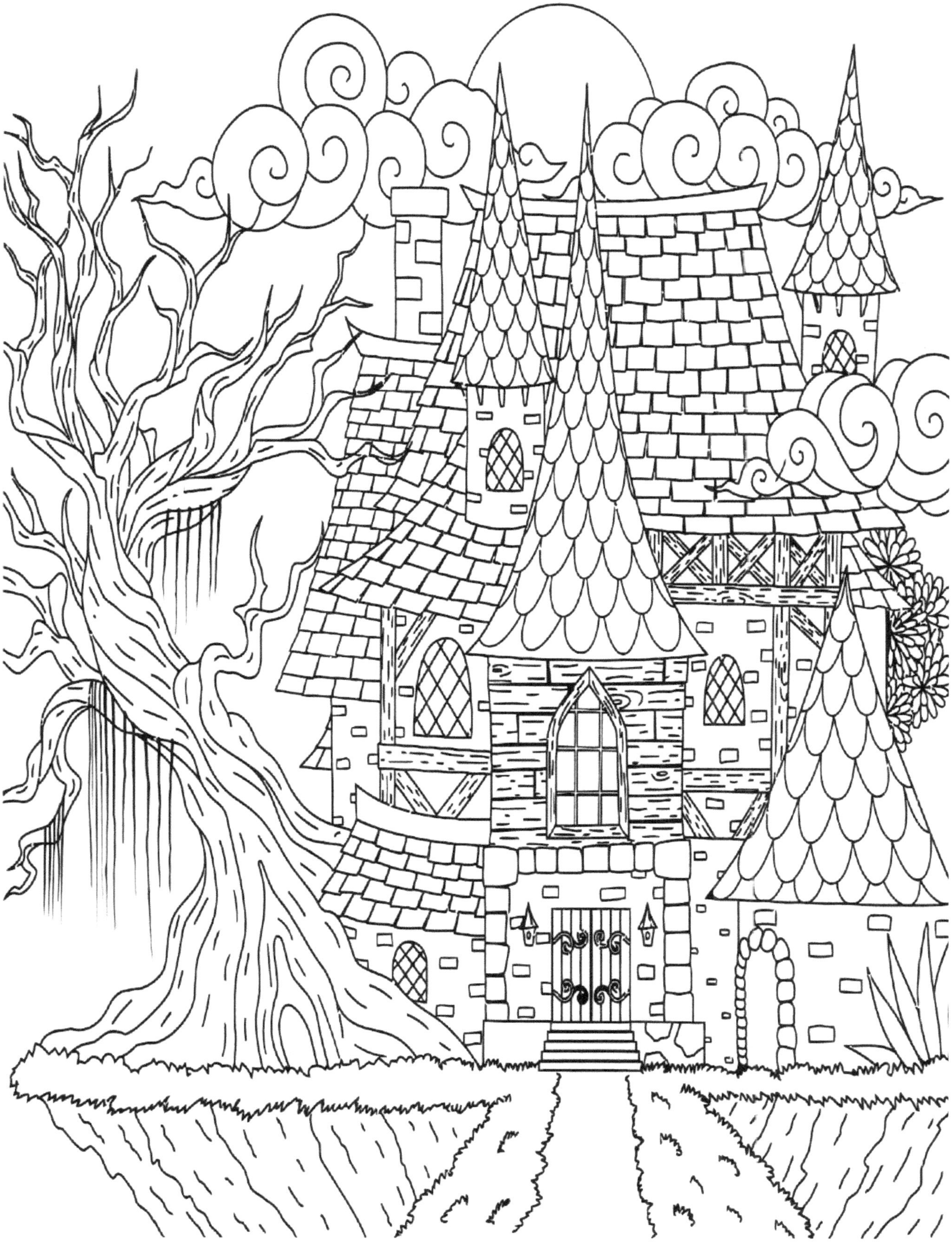

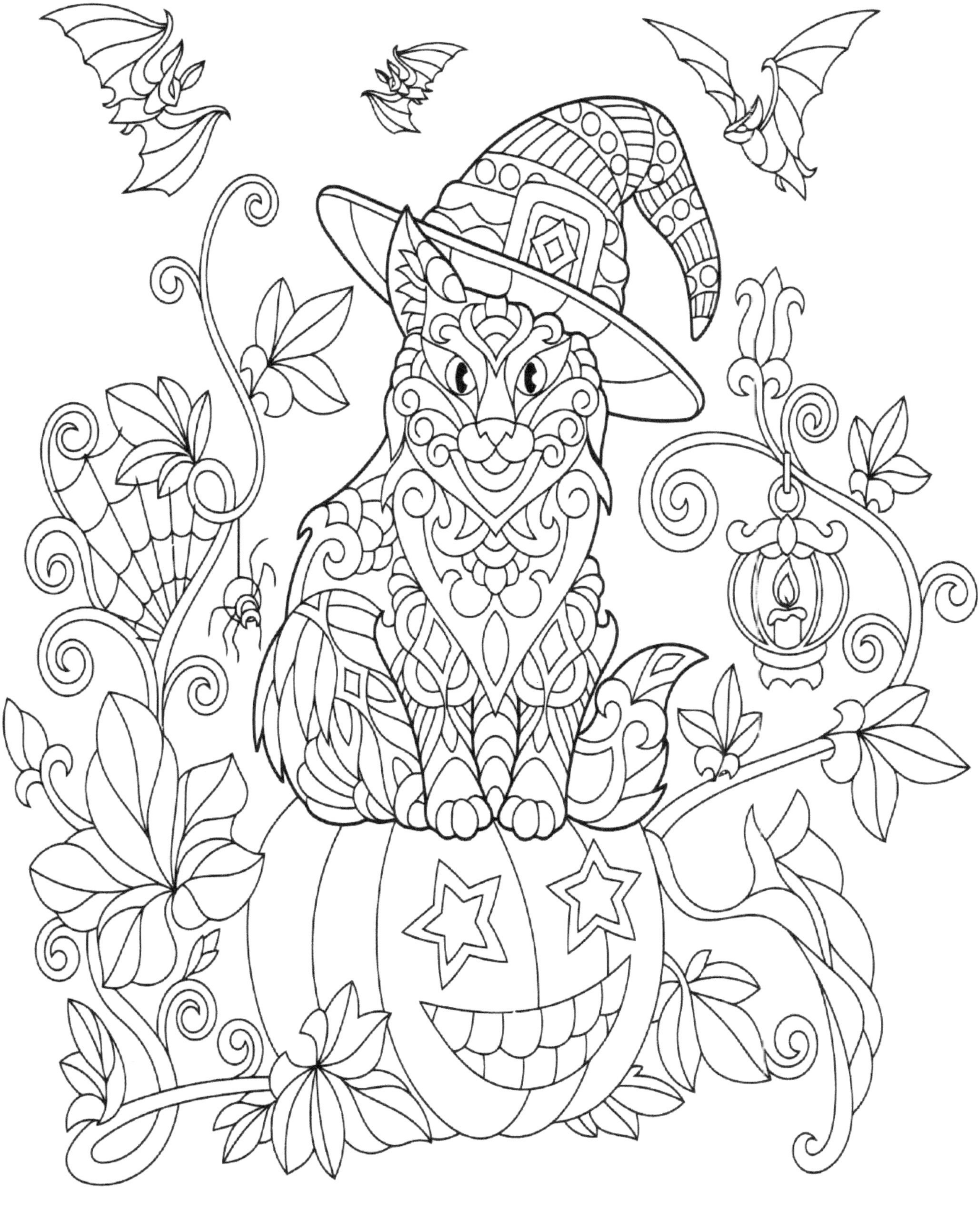

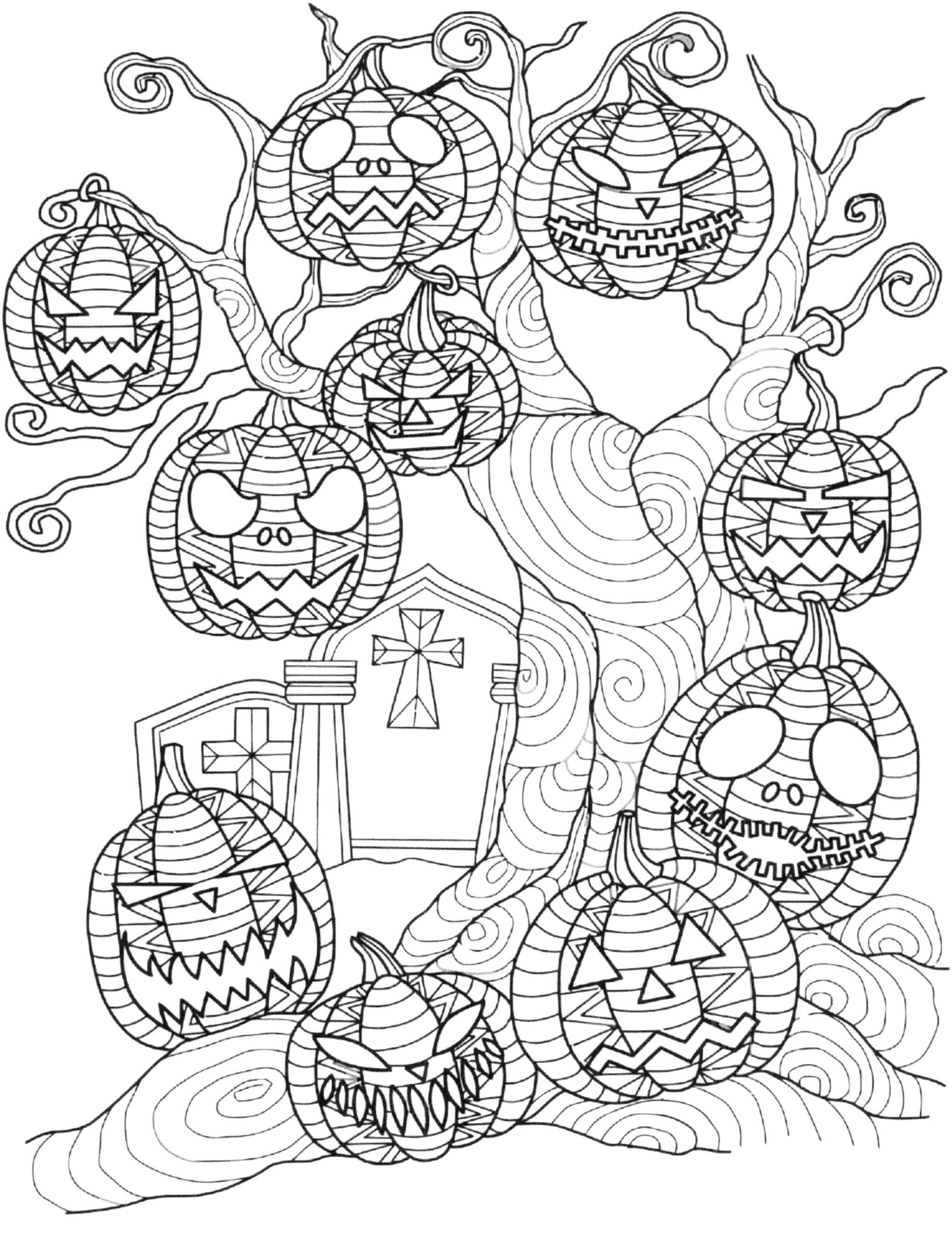

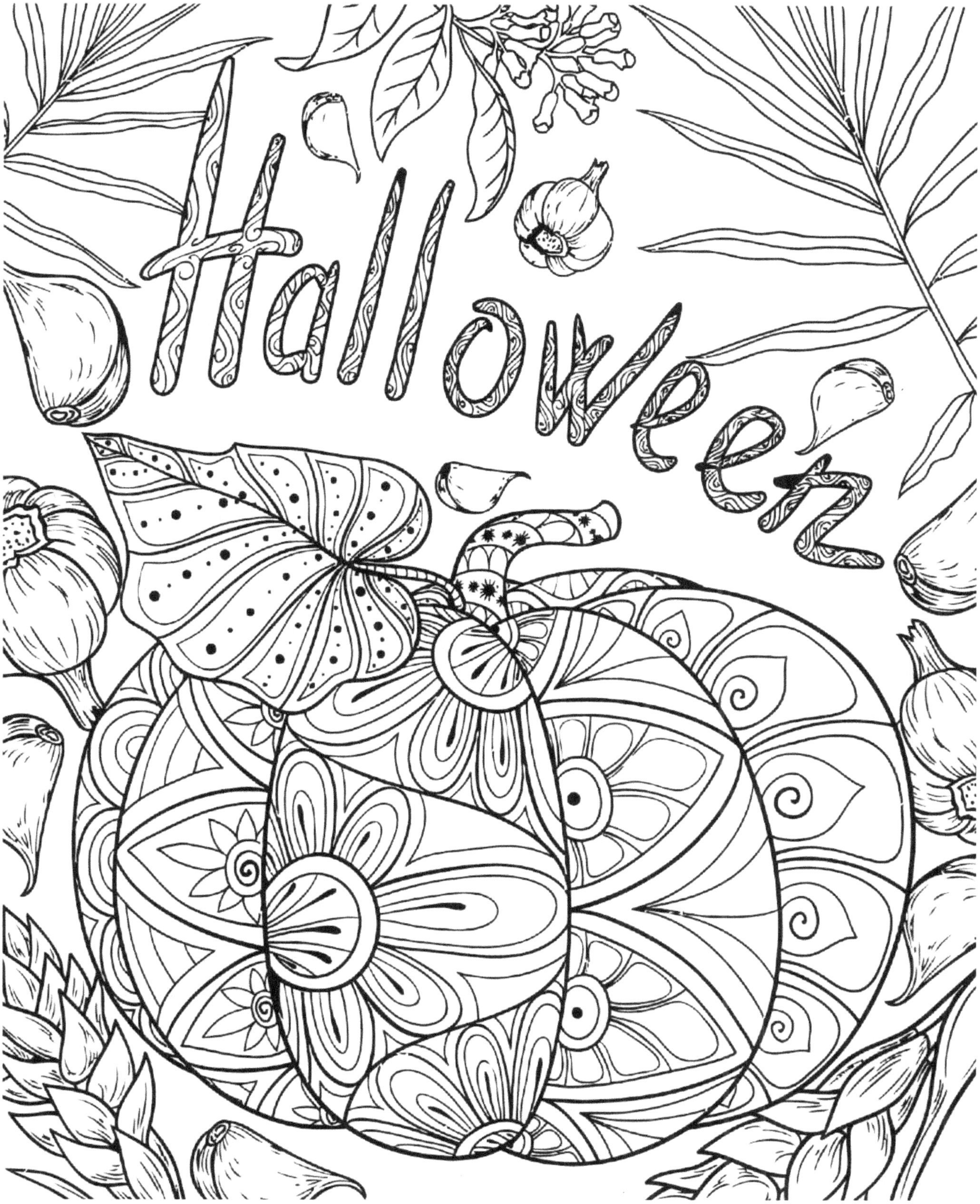
Halloween

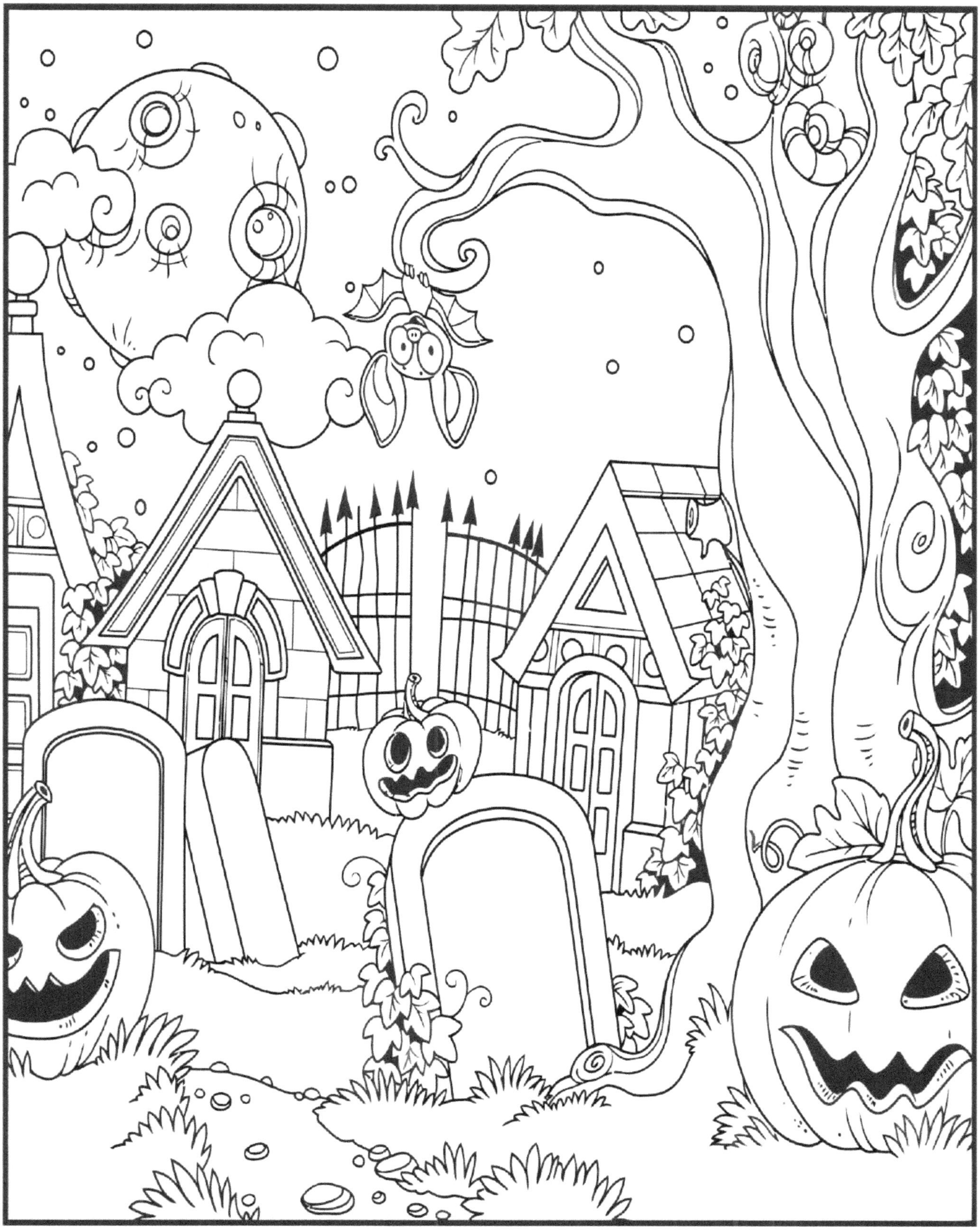

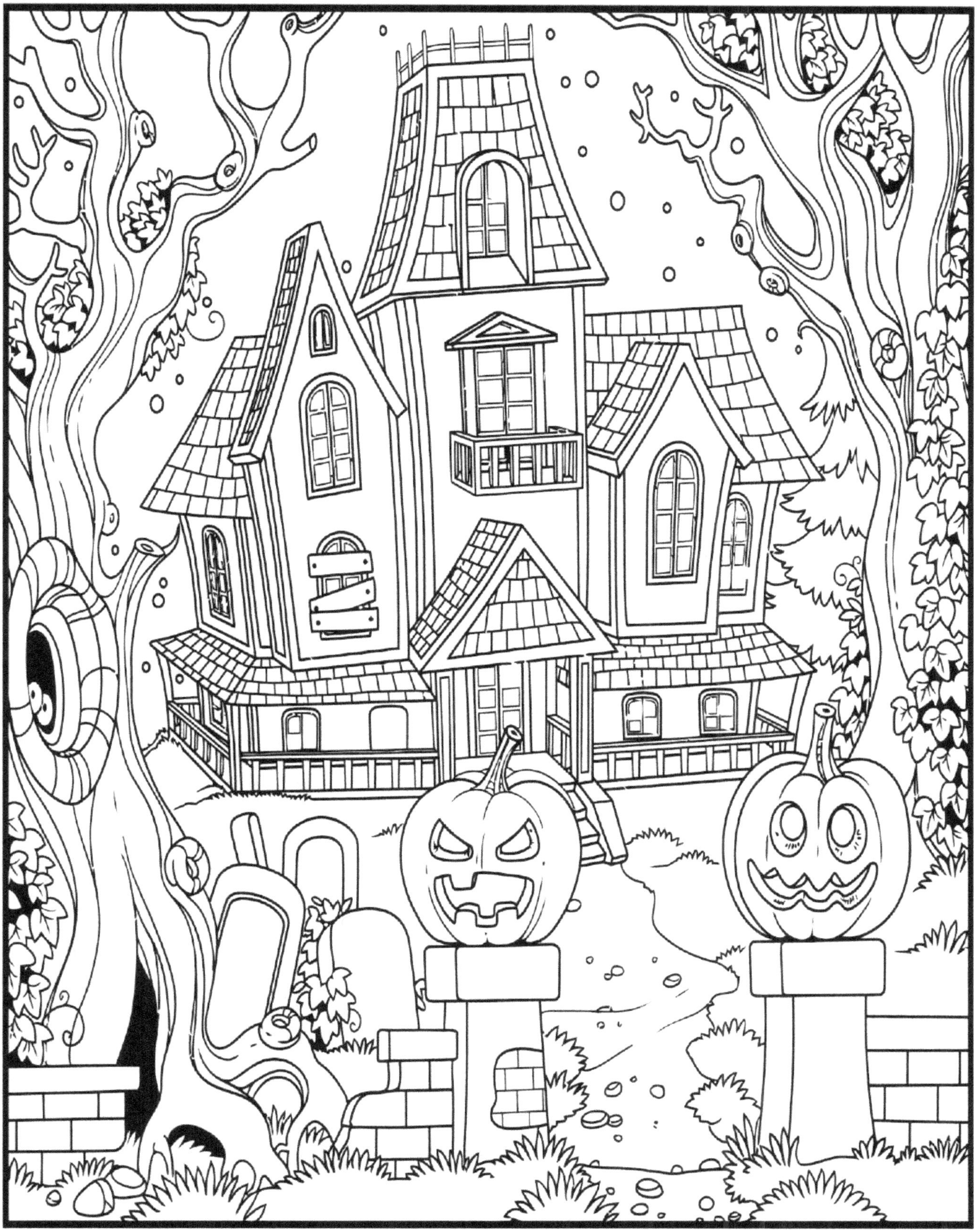

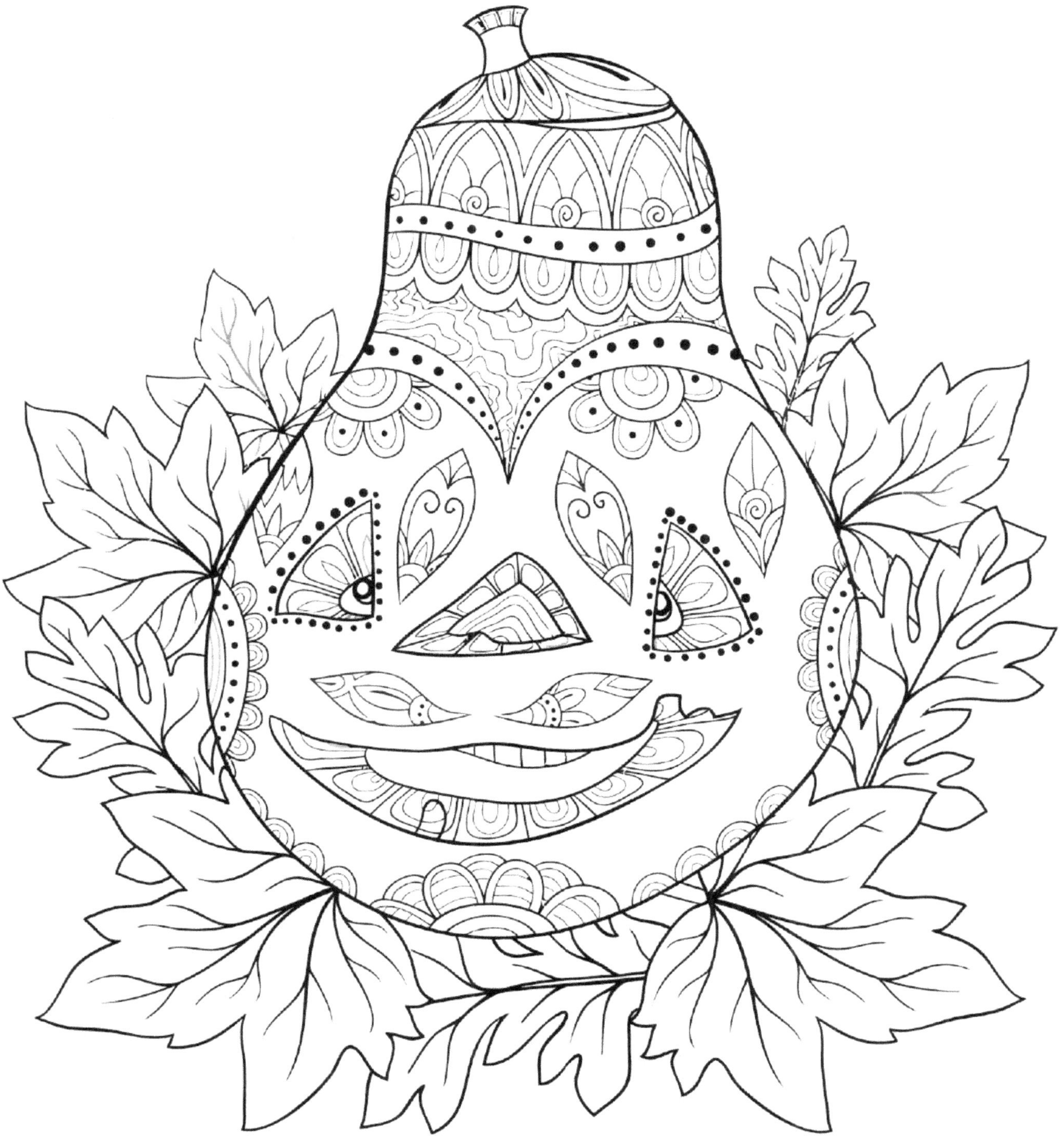

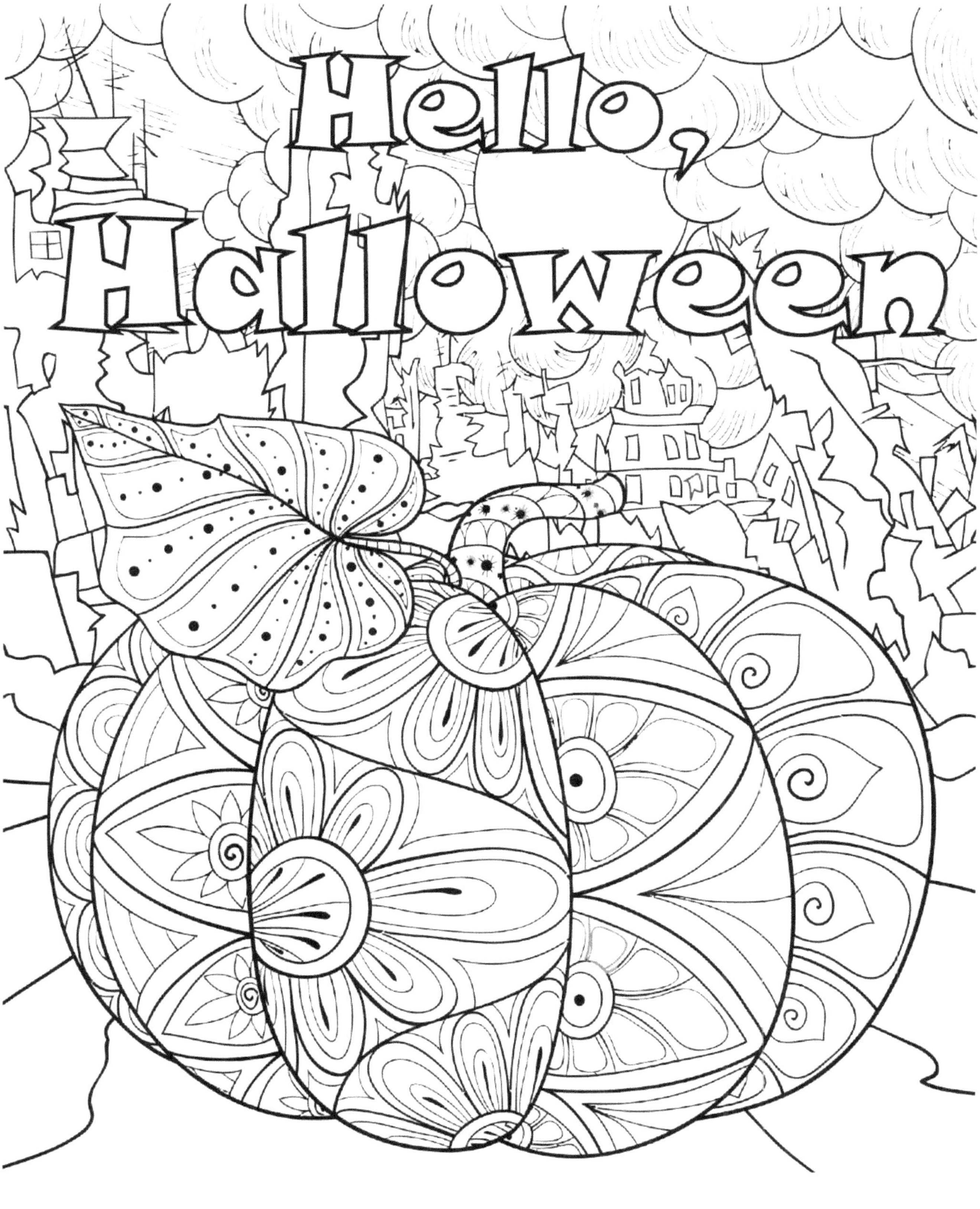
Hello,
Halloween

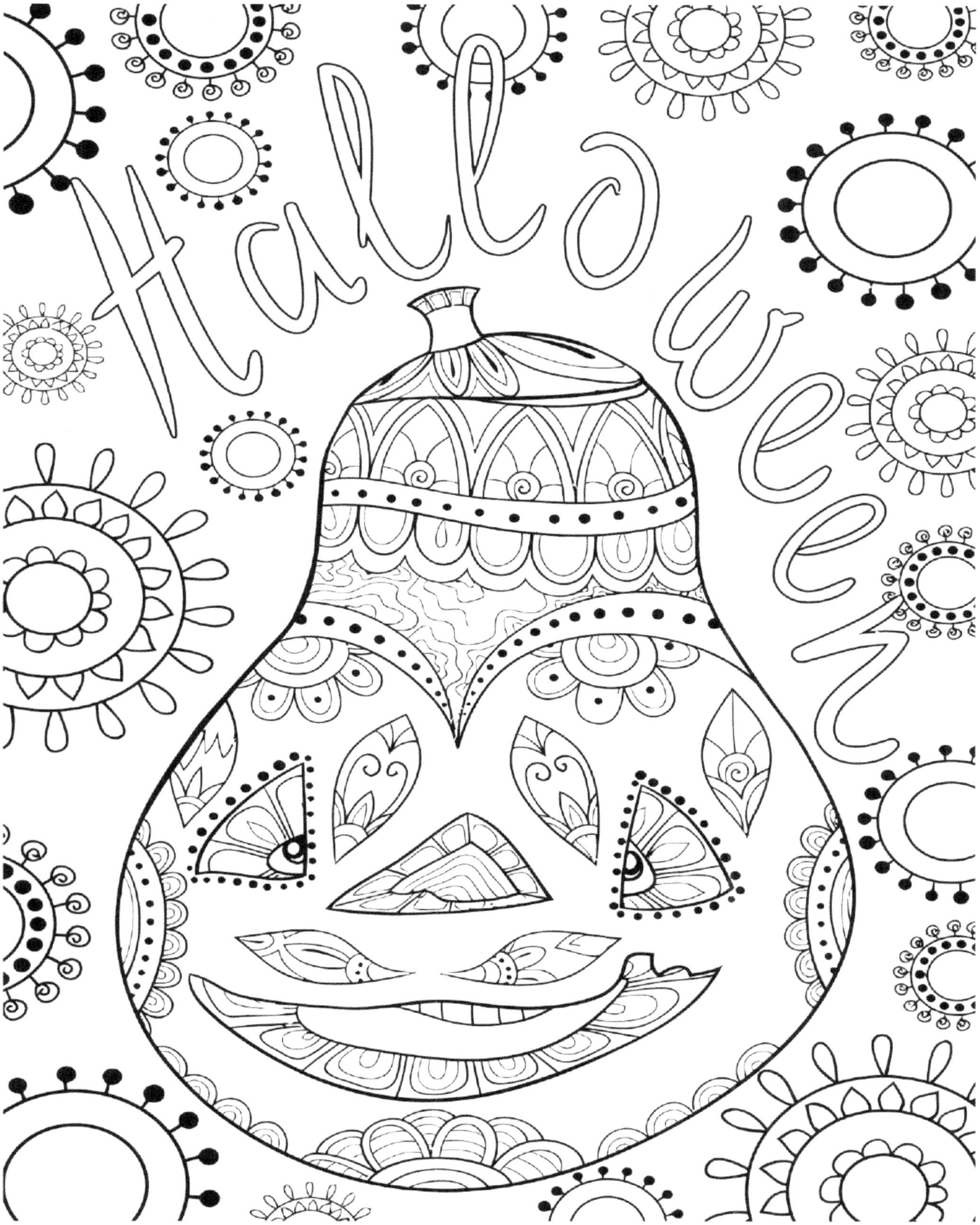
Halloween

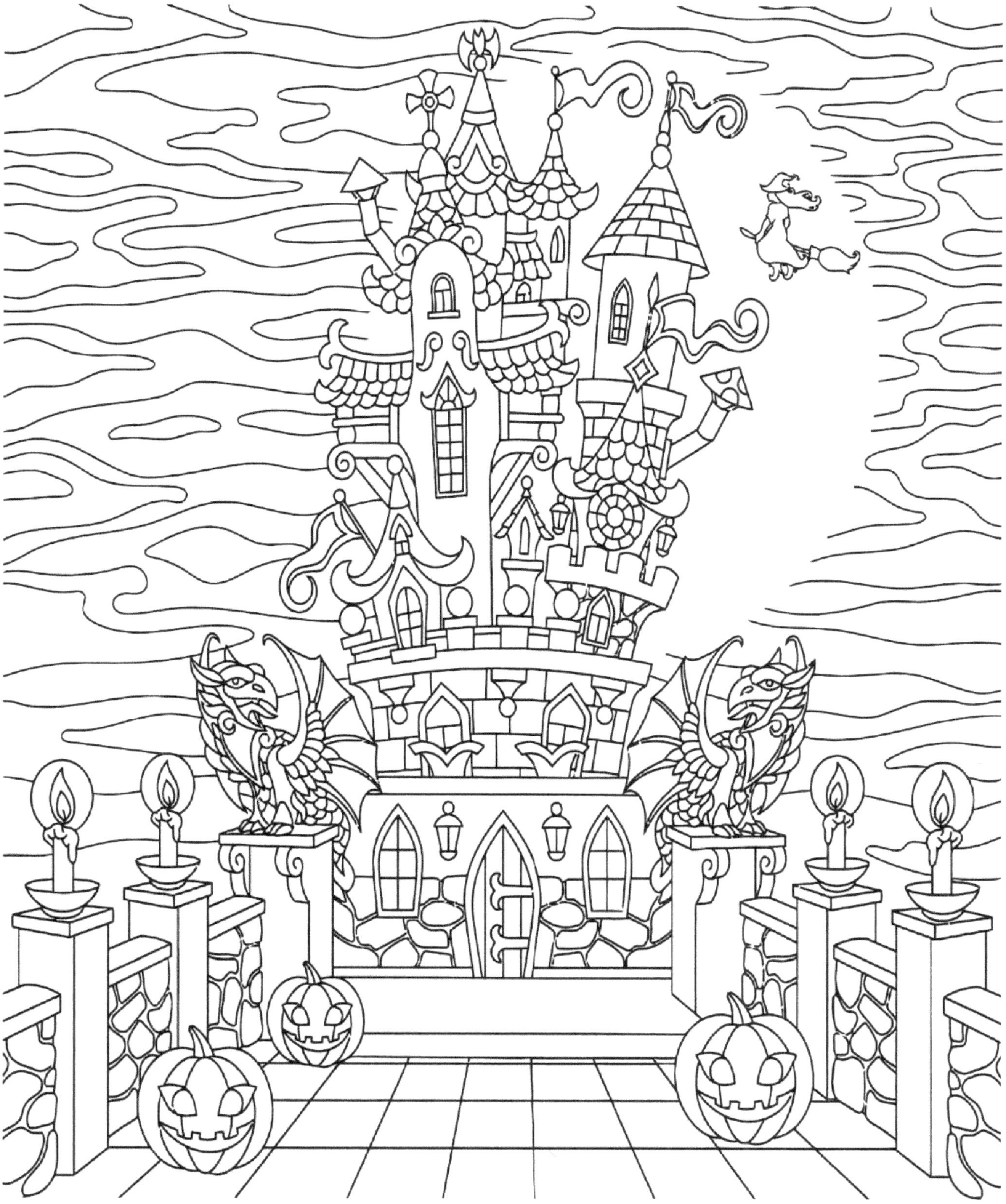

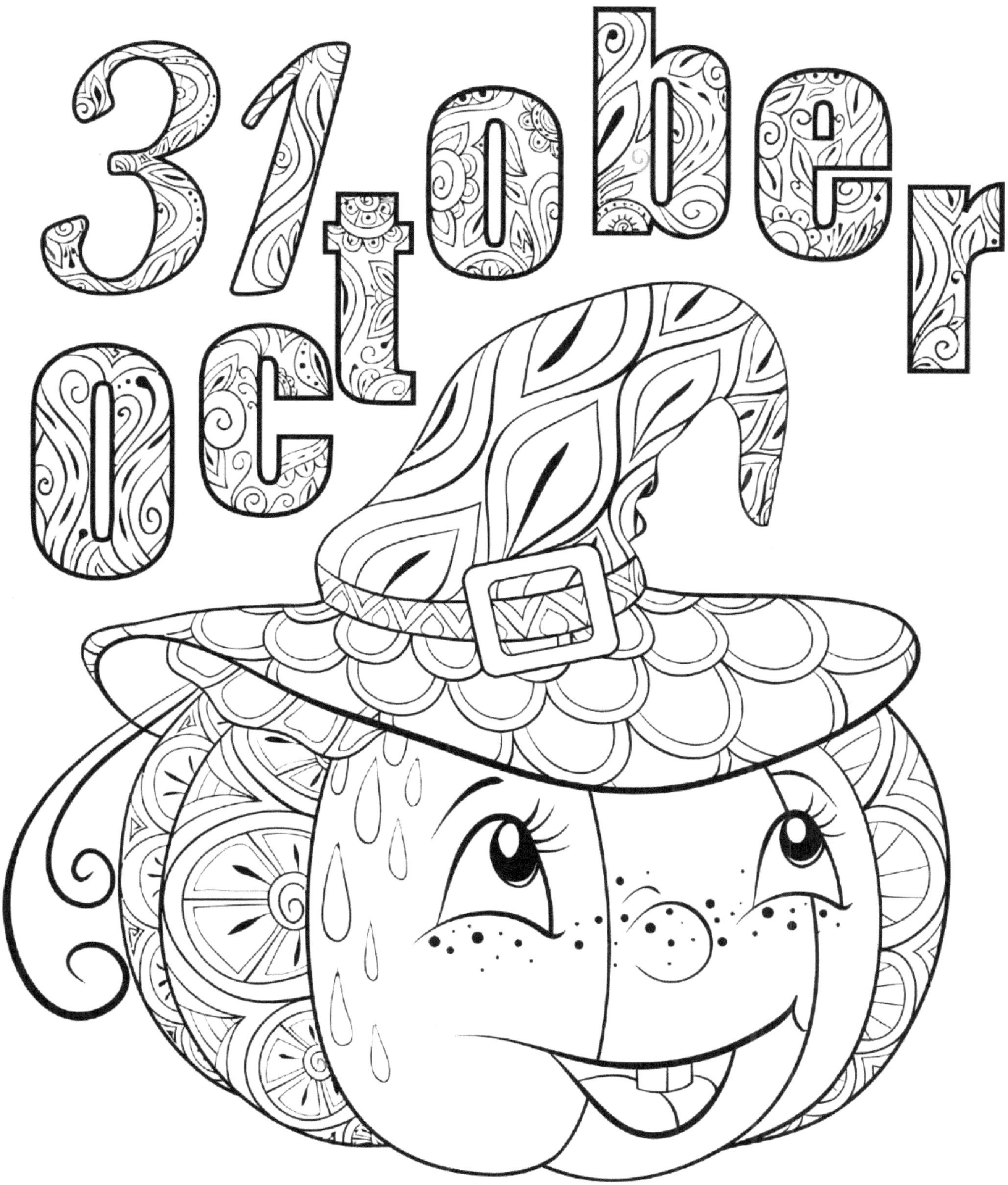
31
October

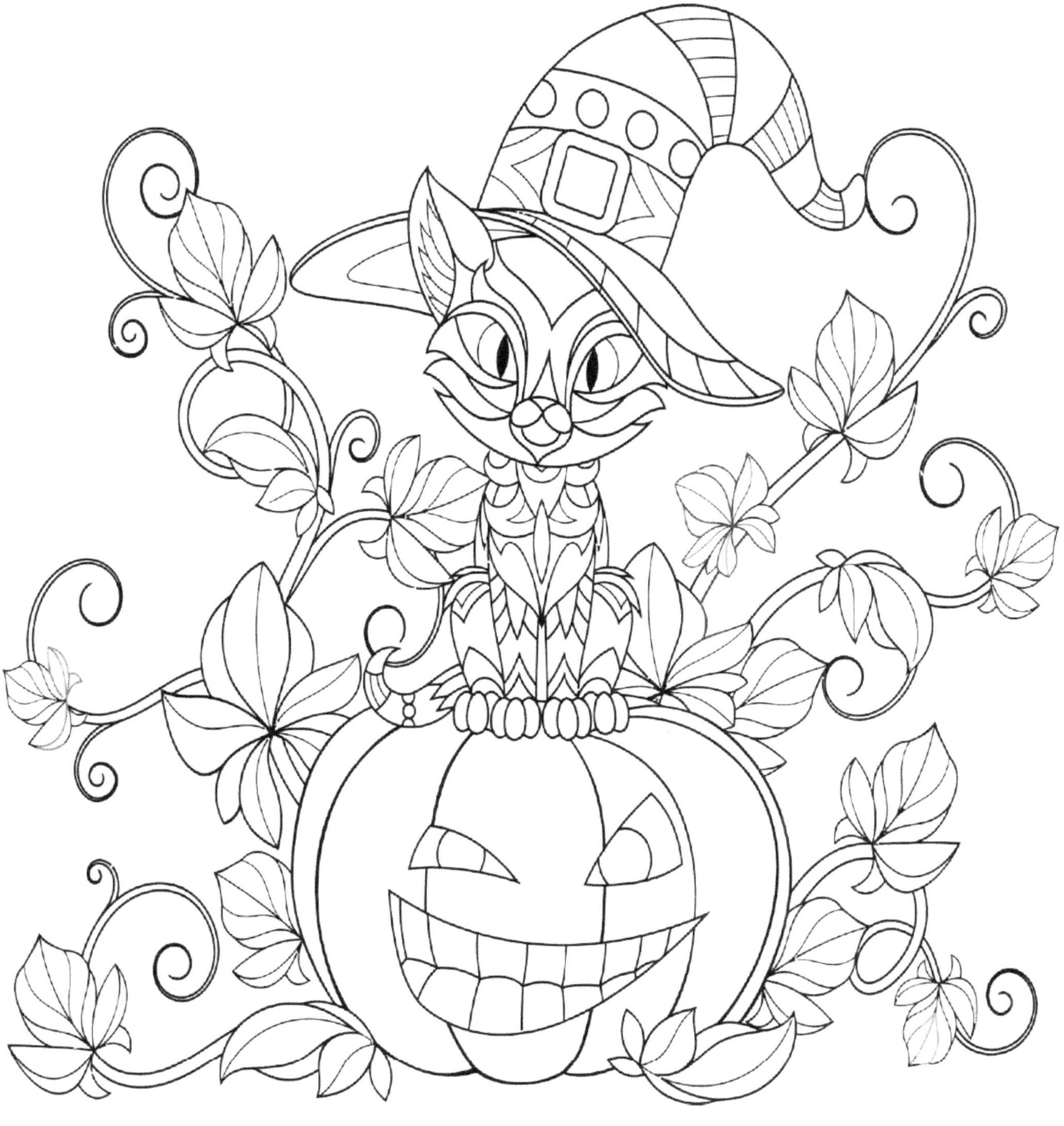

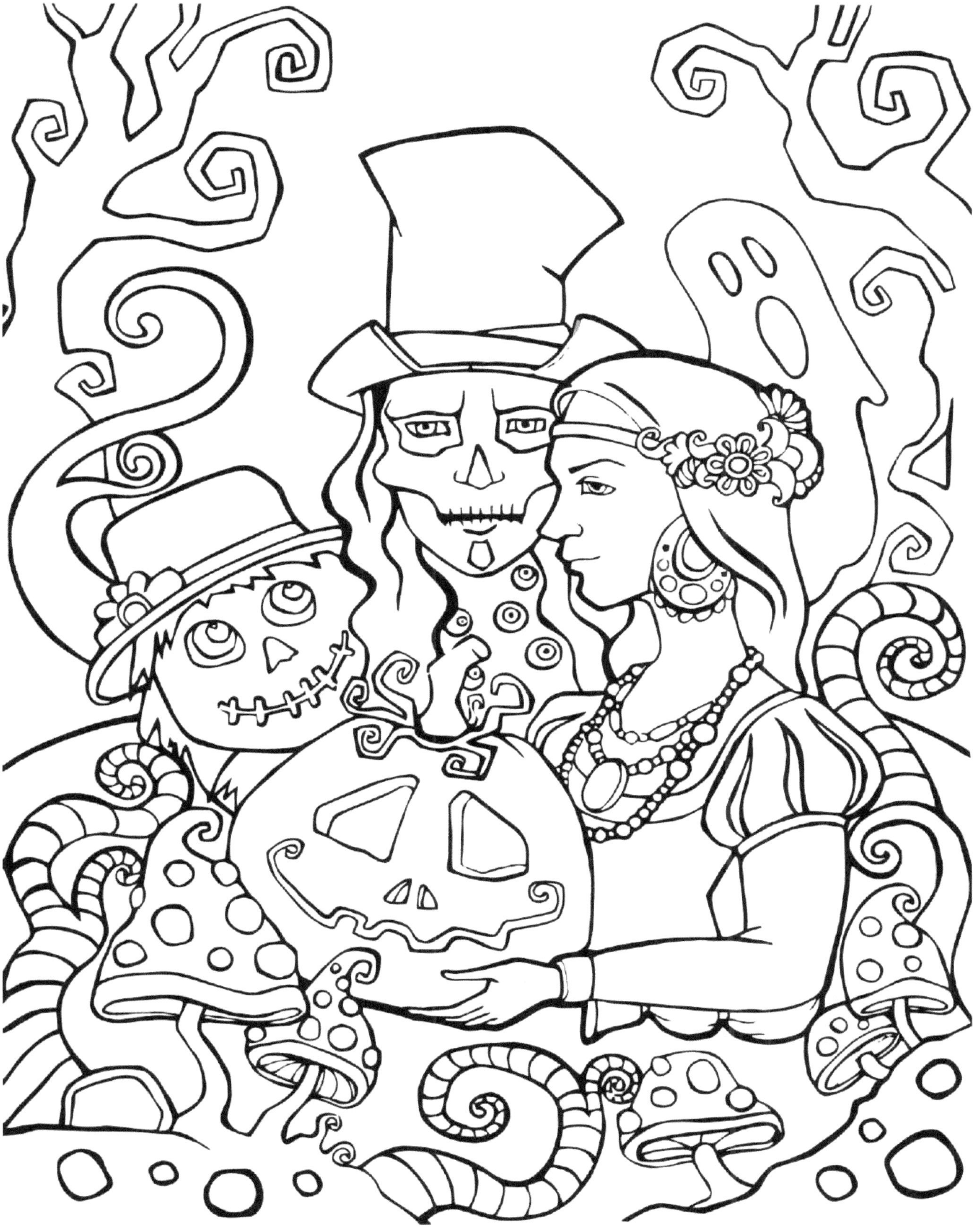

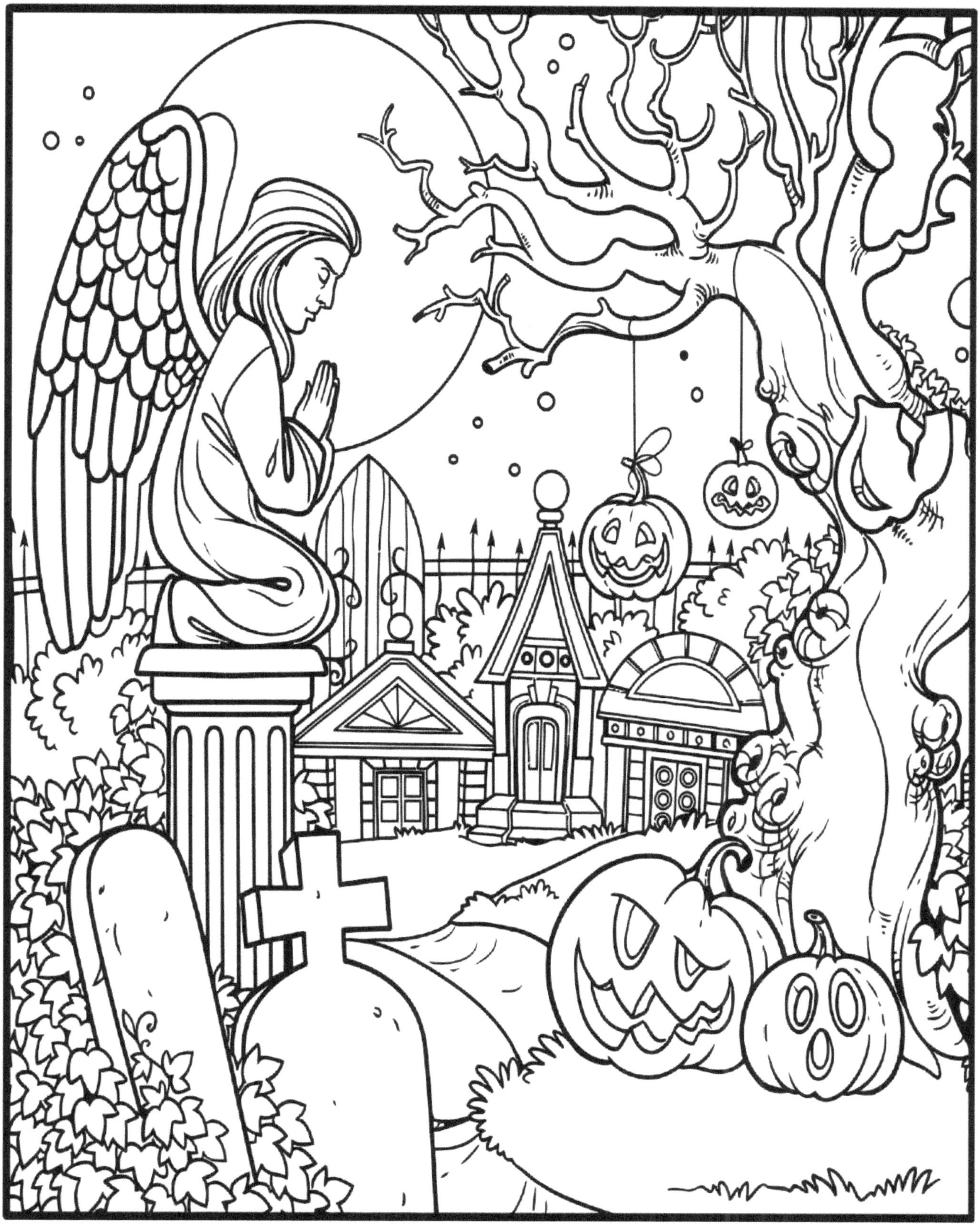

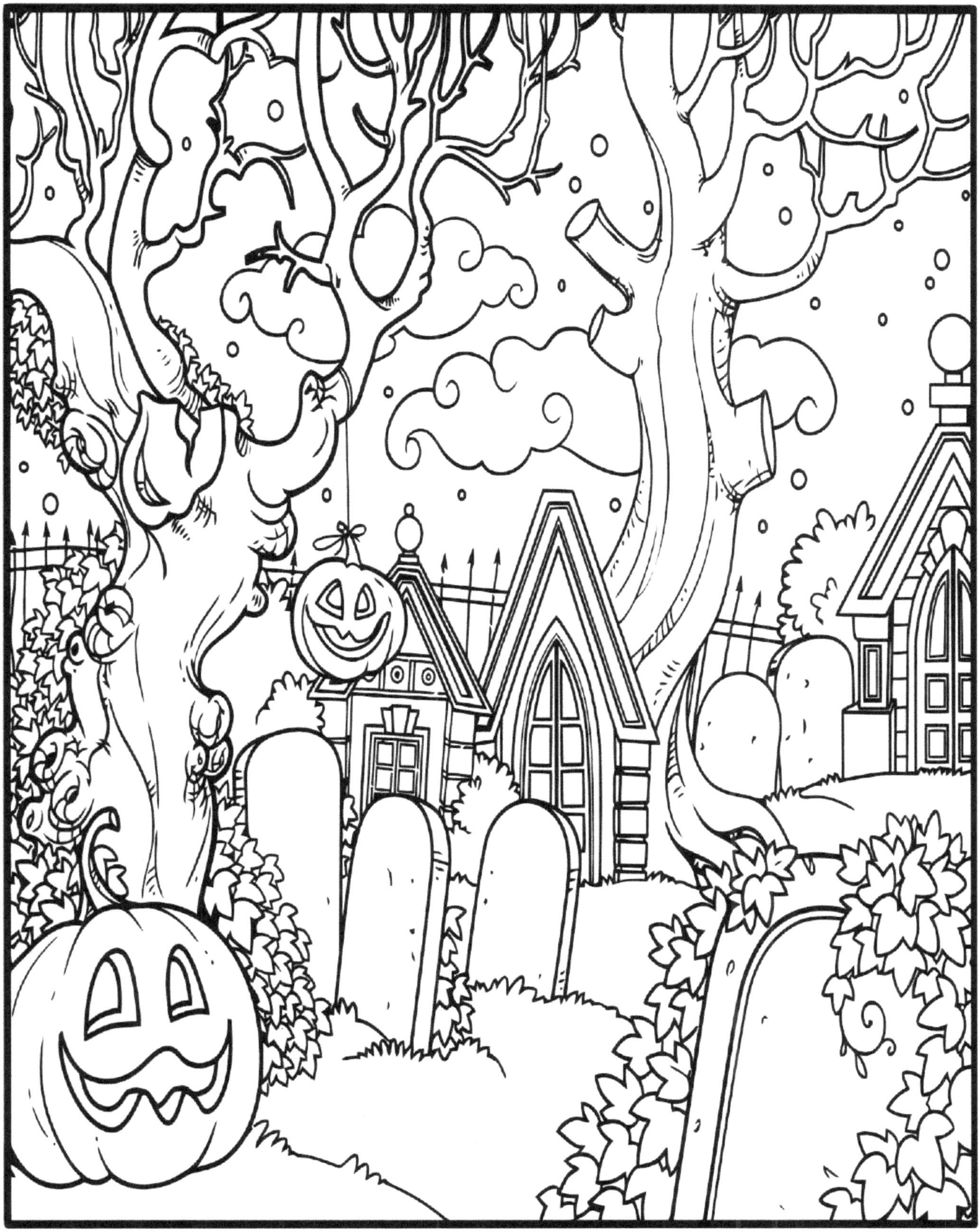

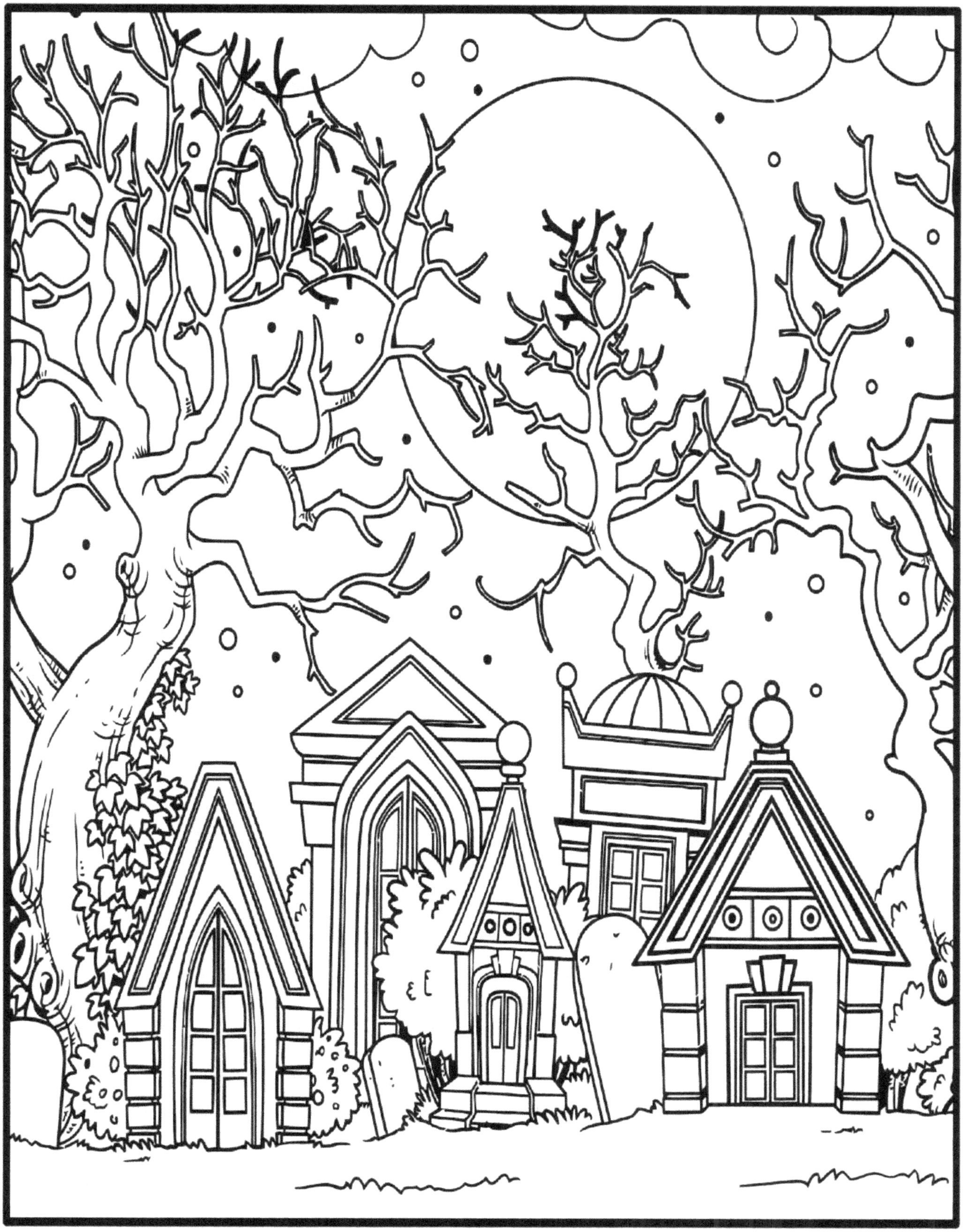

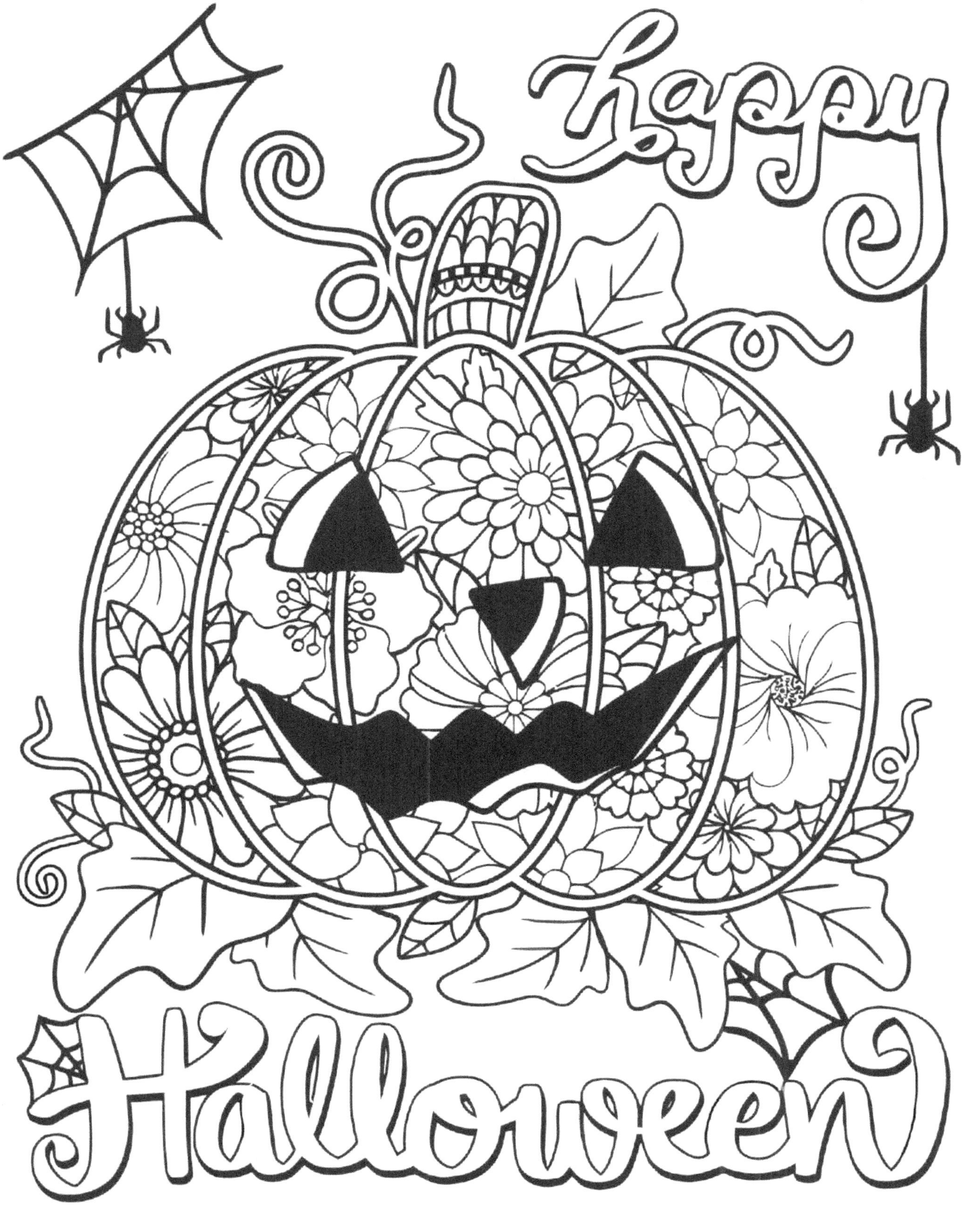
happy
Halloween

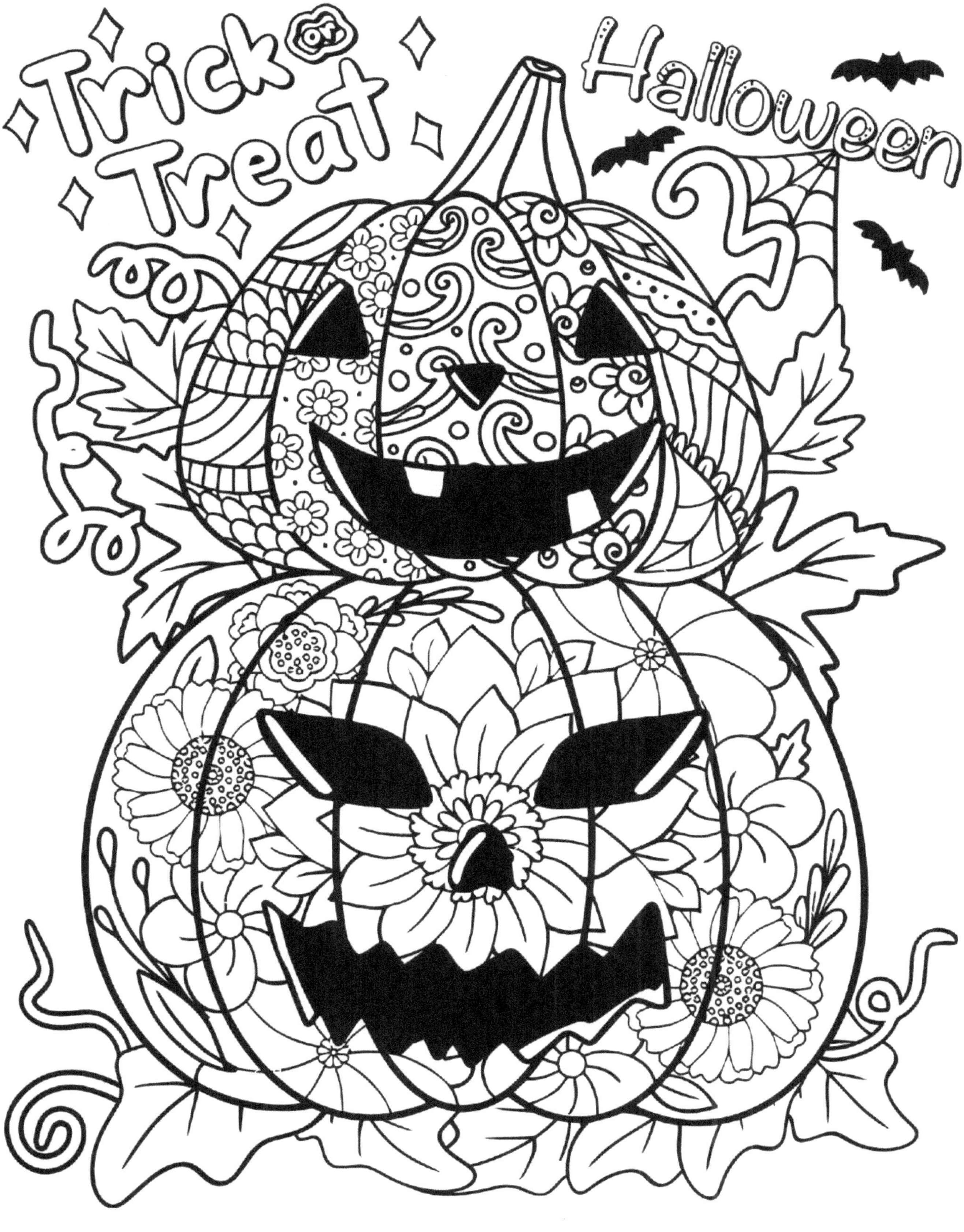

Trick or Treat
Halloween

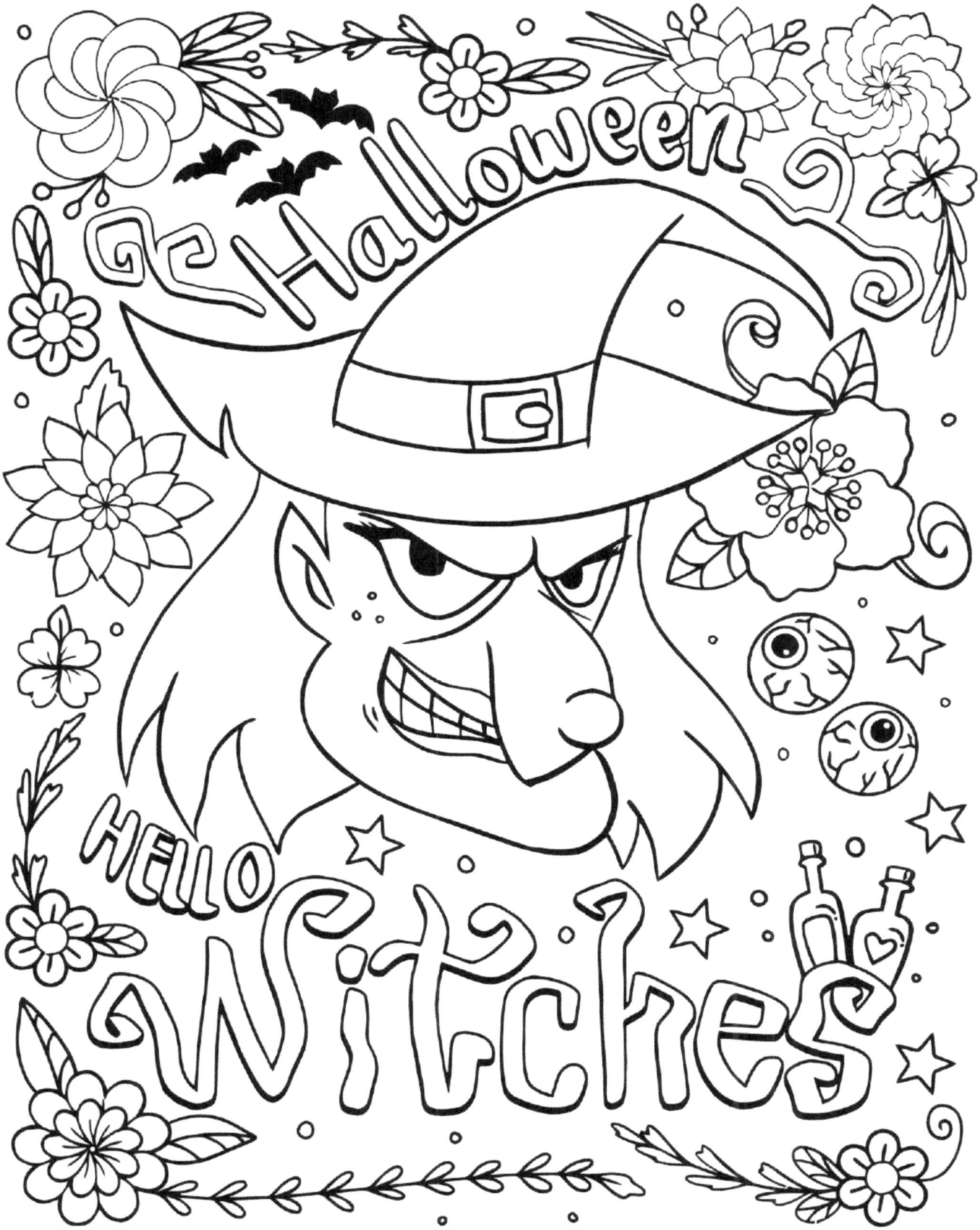
Halloween
HELLO
Witches

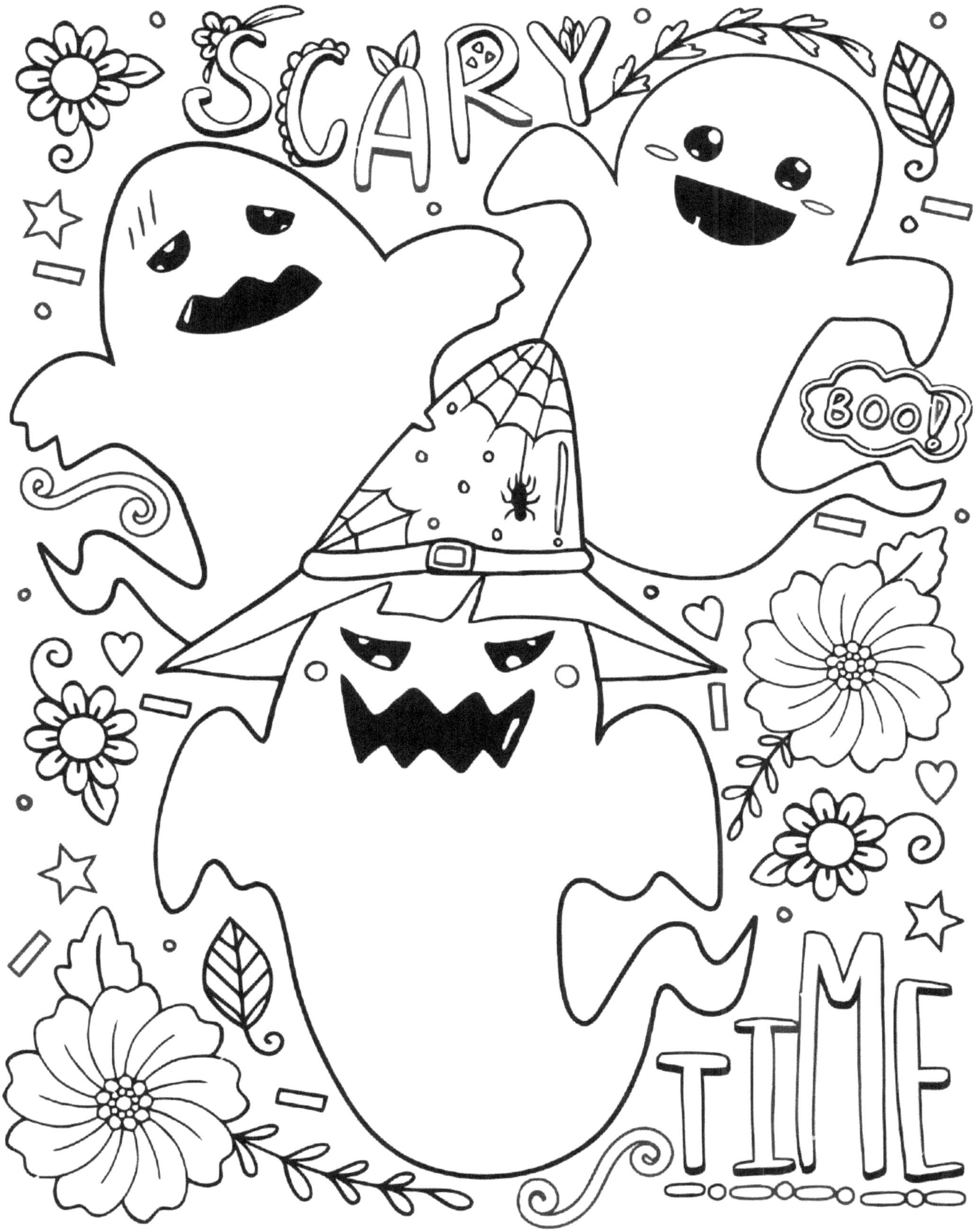
SCARY
BOO!
TIME

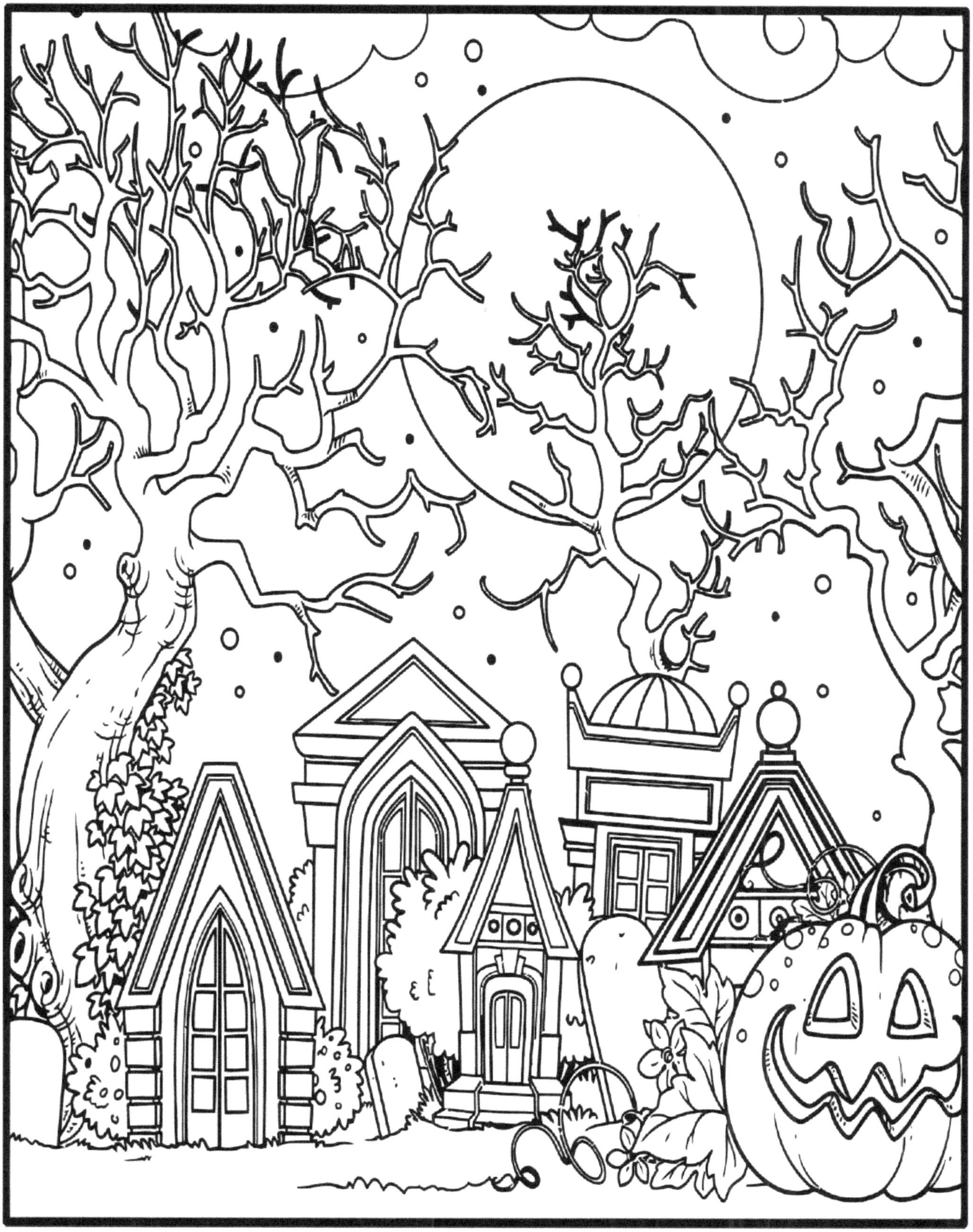

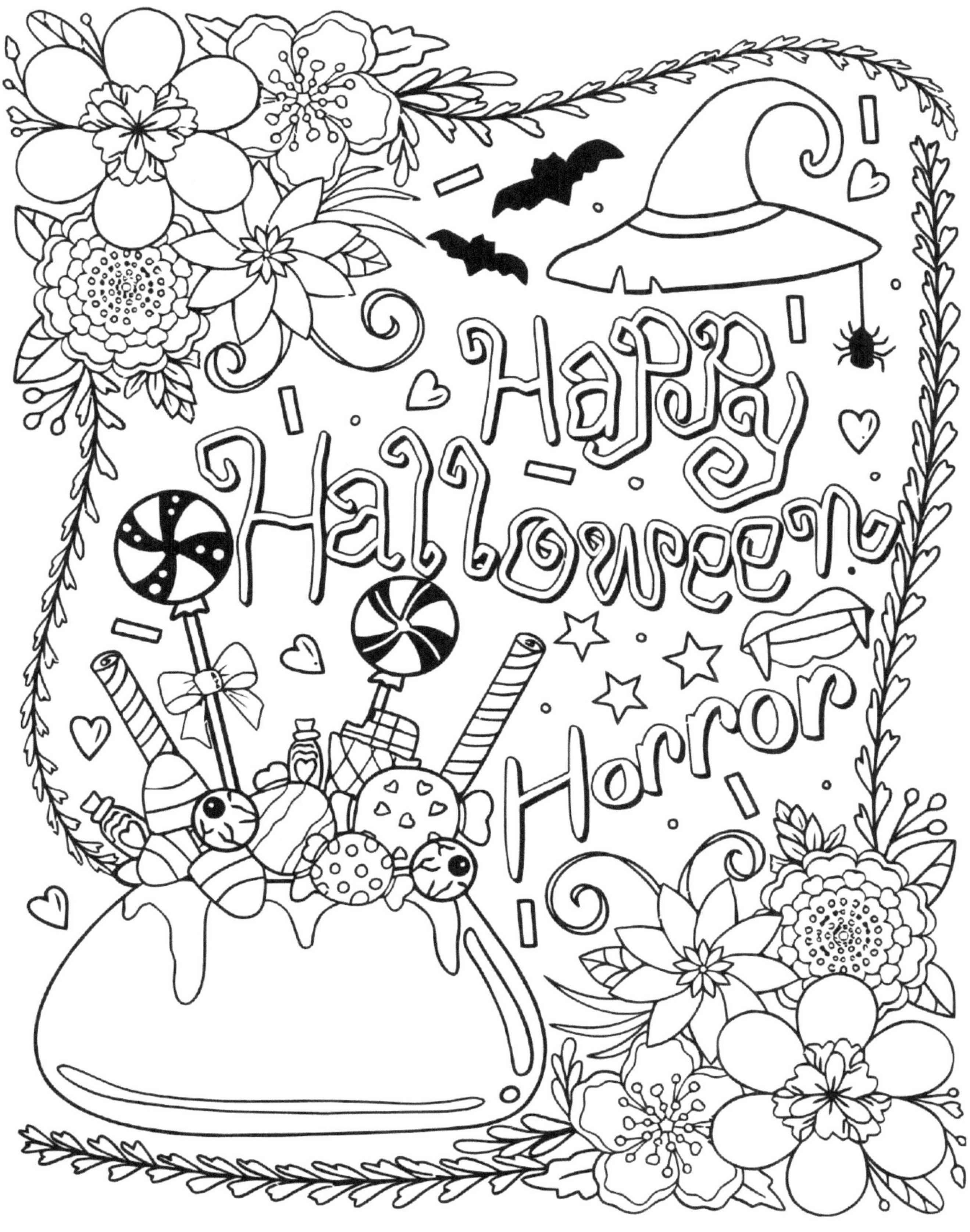
Happy
Halloween
Horror

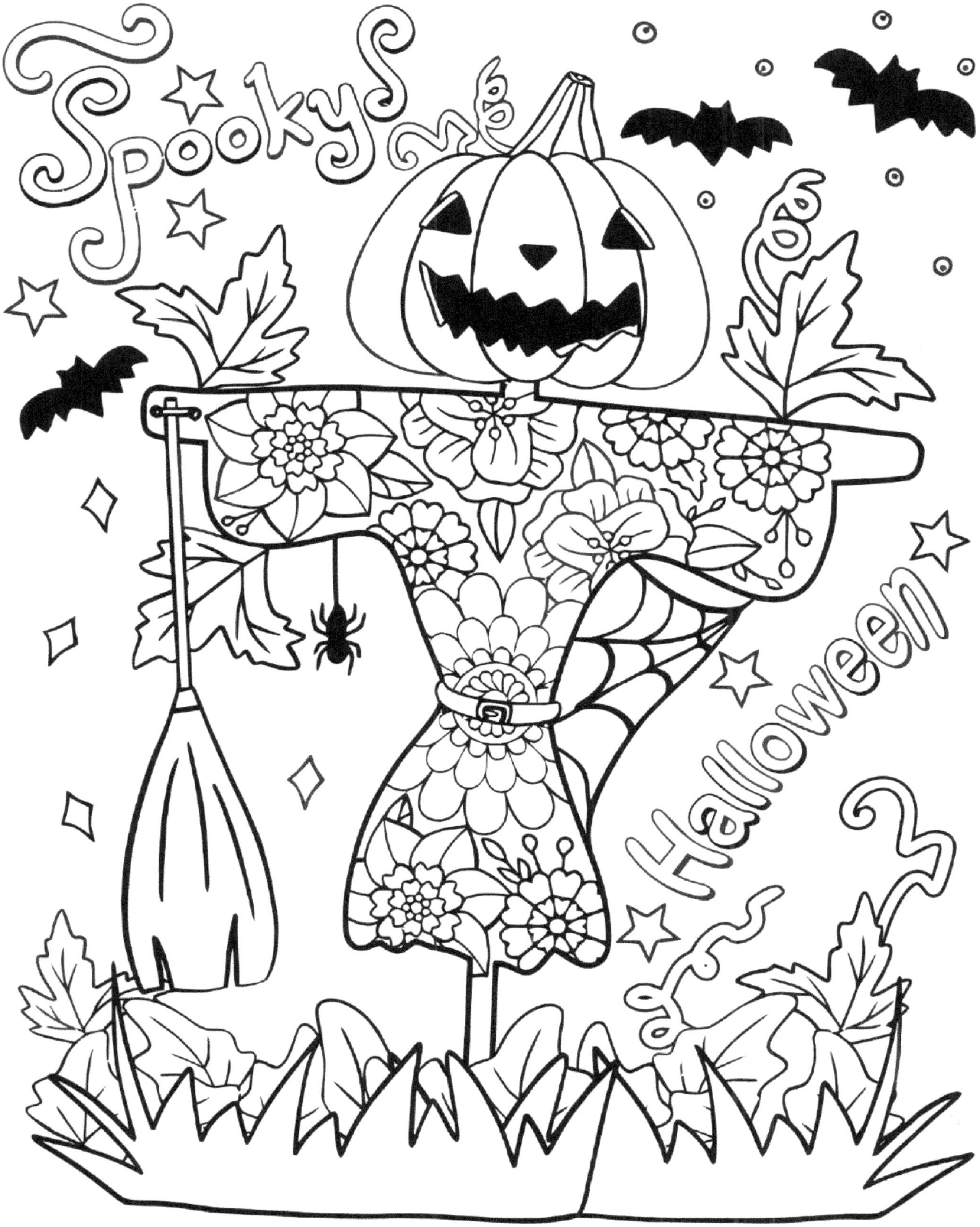
Spooky
Halloween

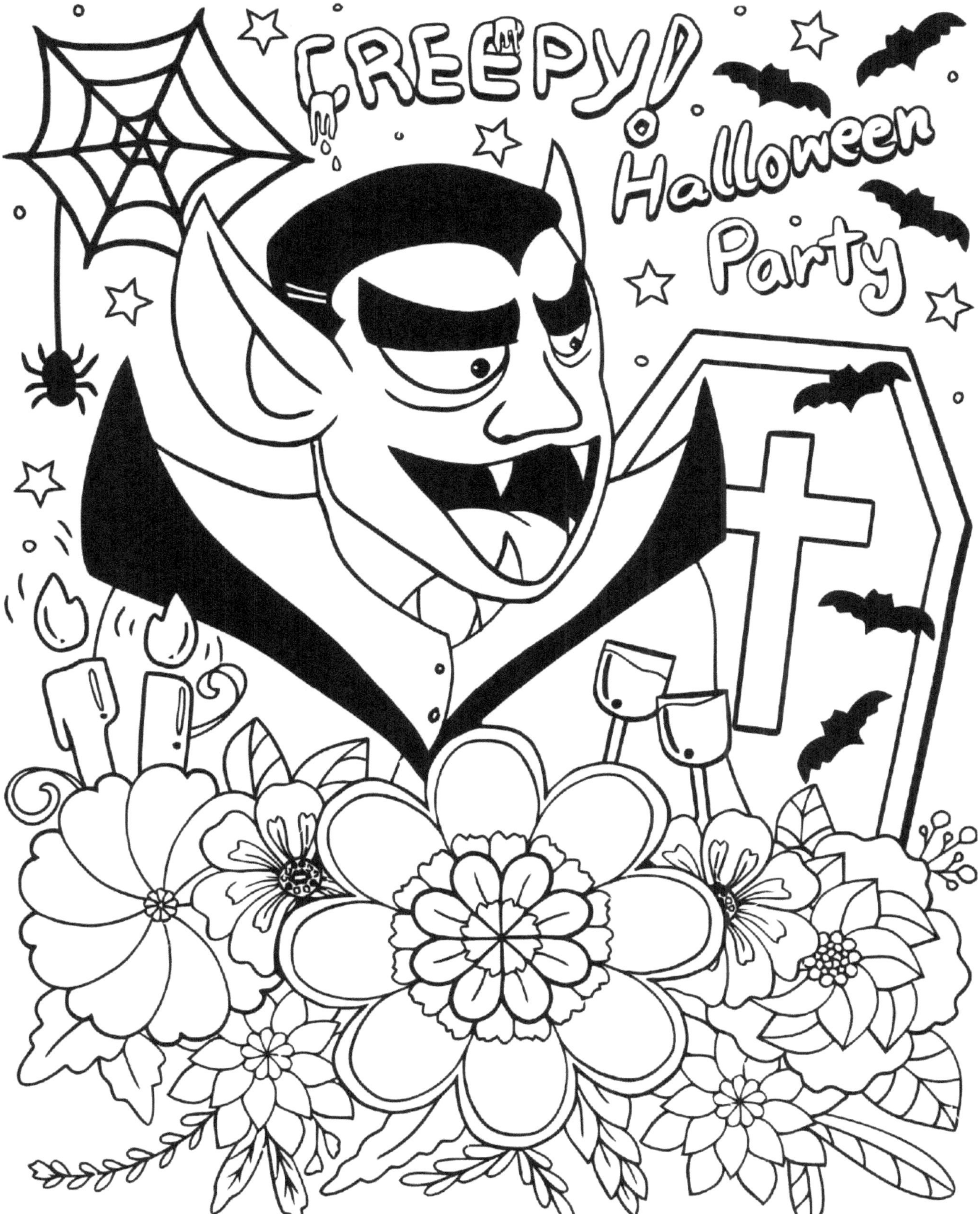

CREEPY!
Halloween
Party

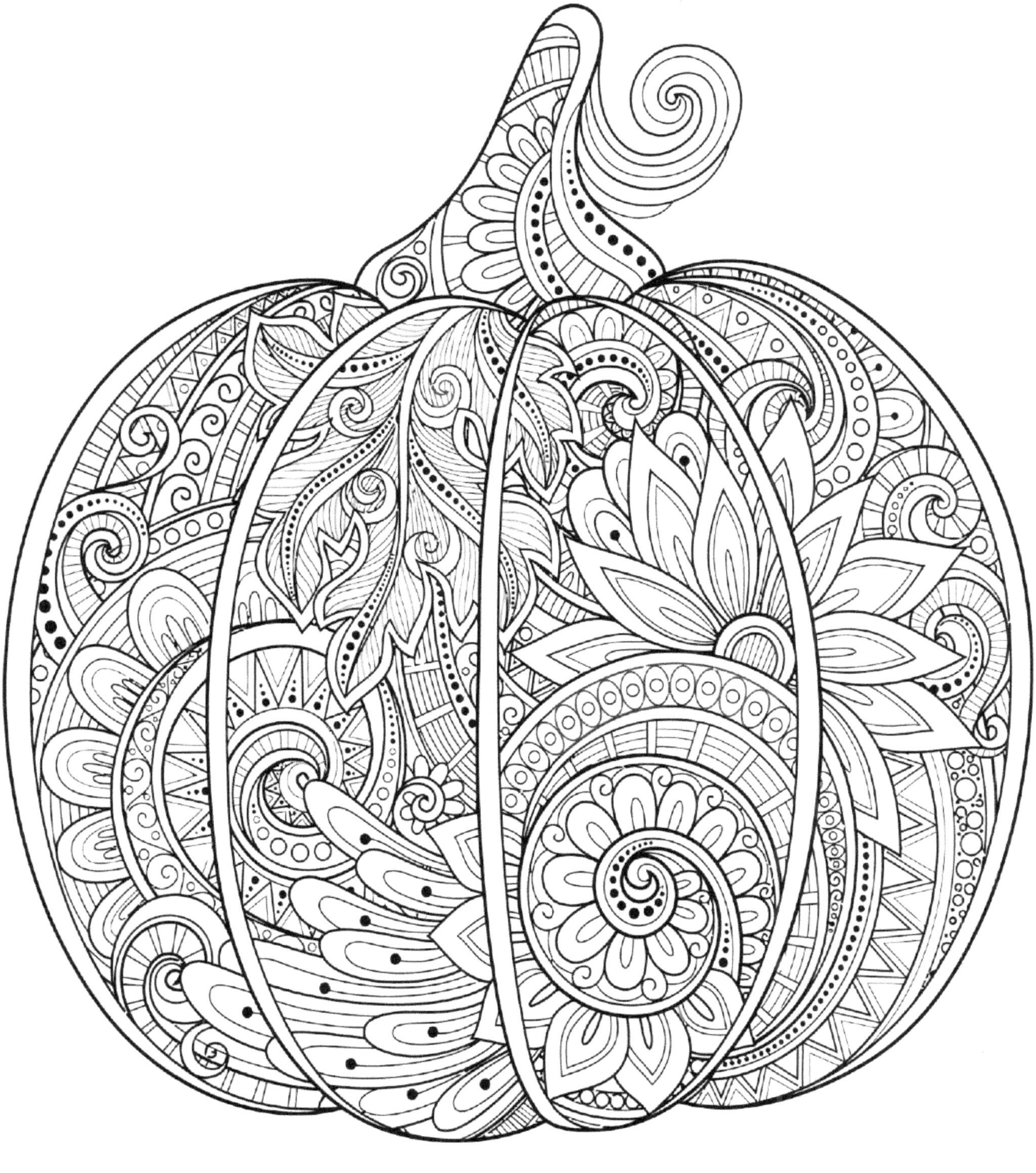

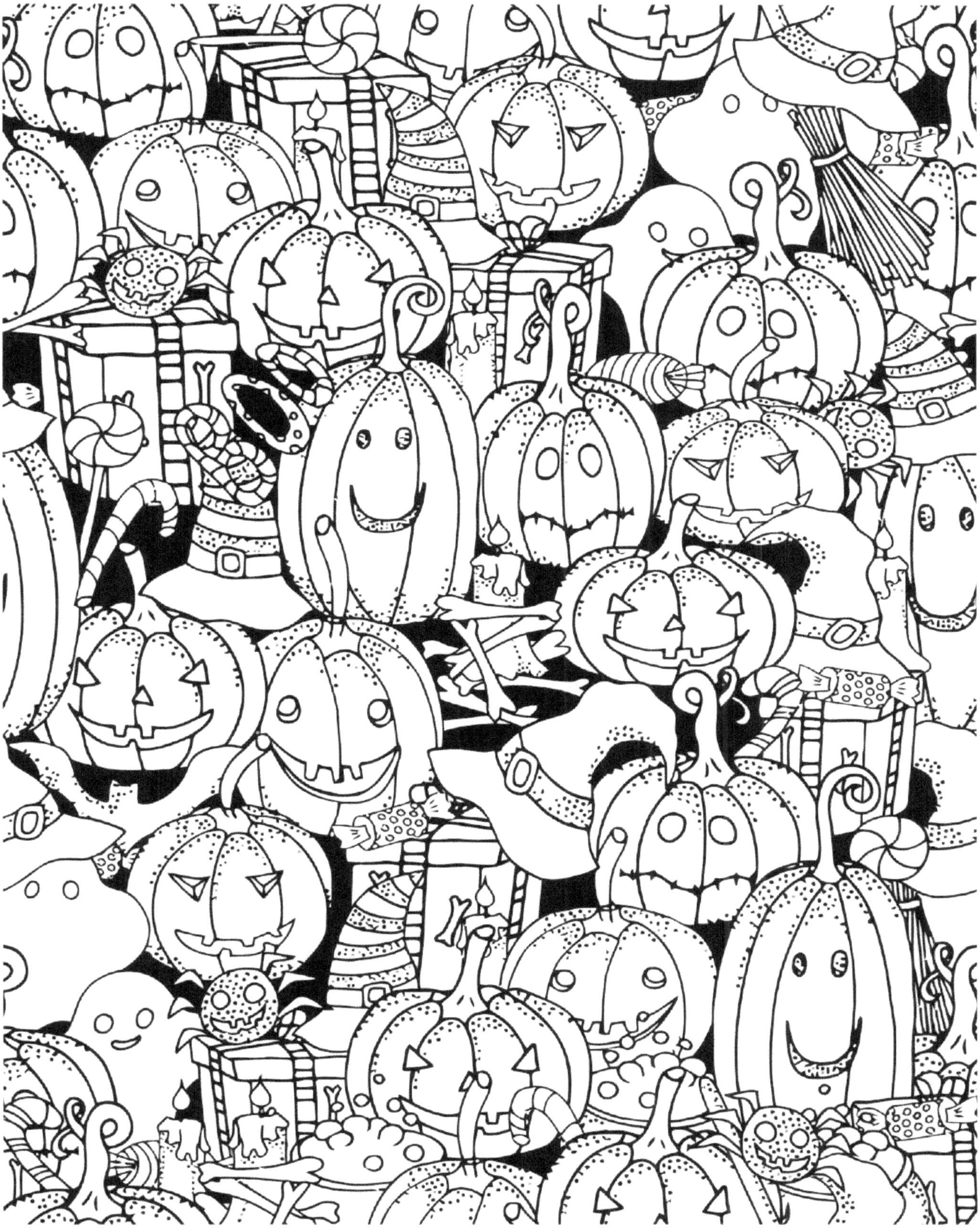

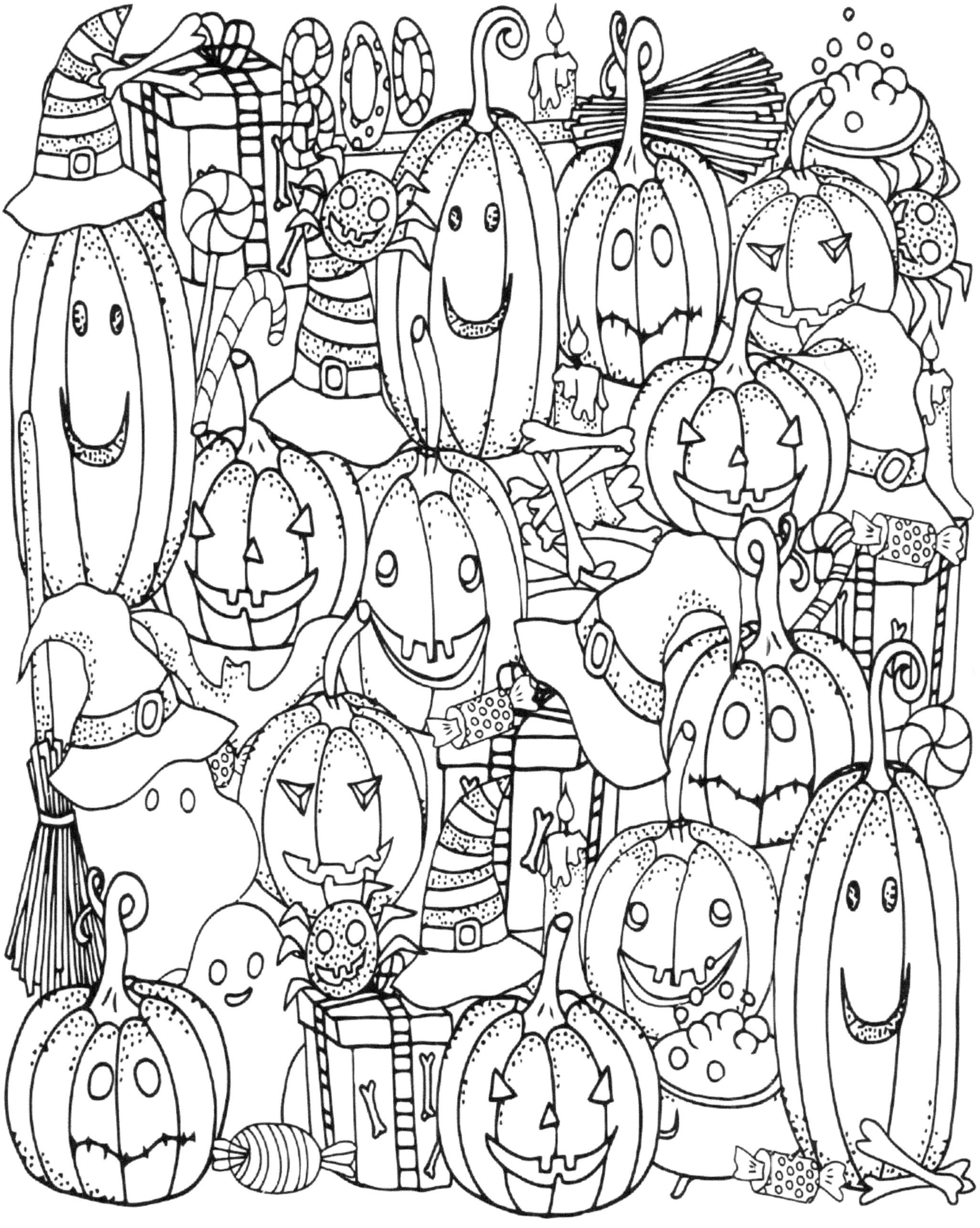
BOO

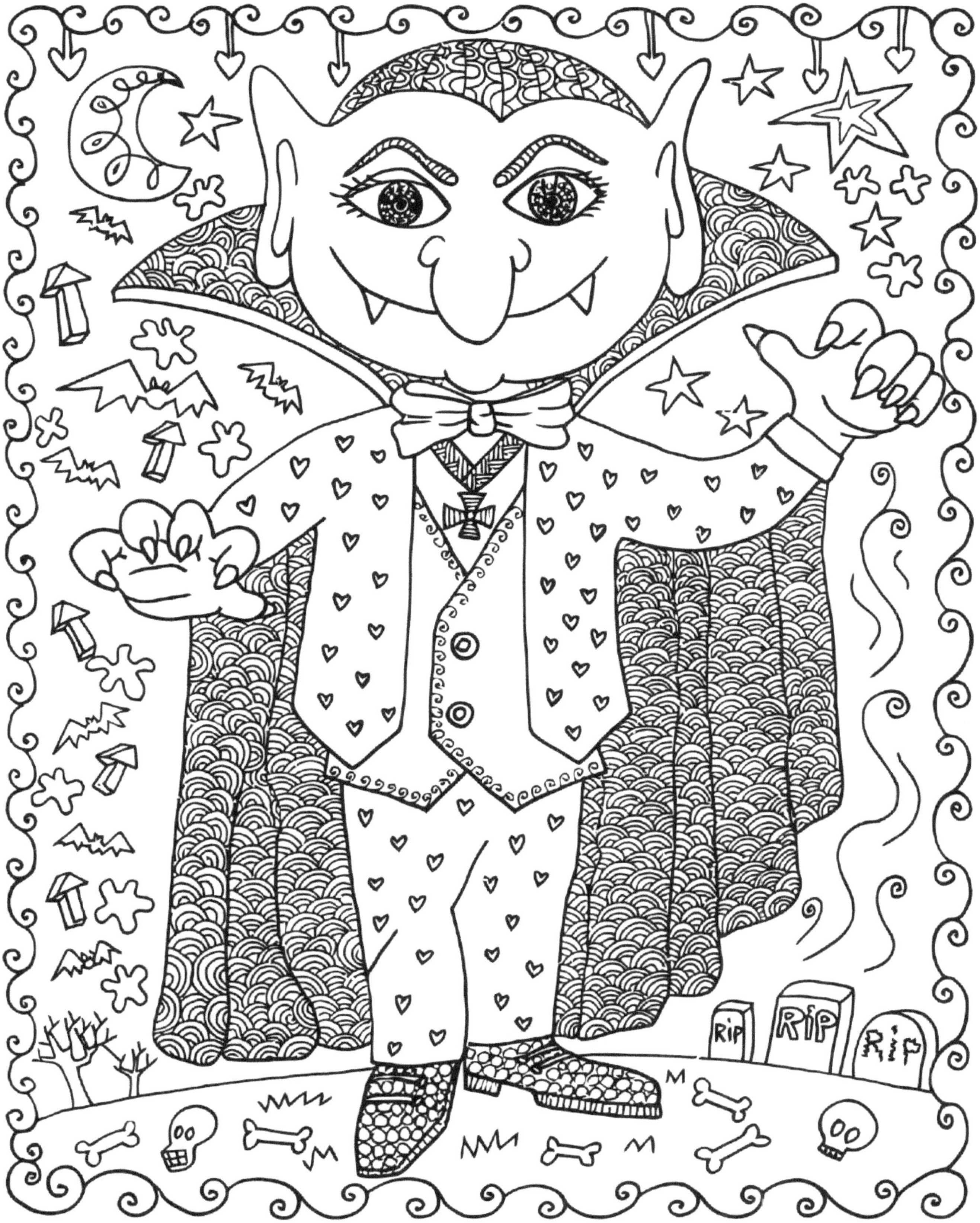
RIP
RIP
RIP

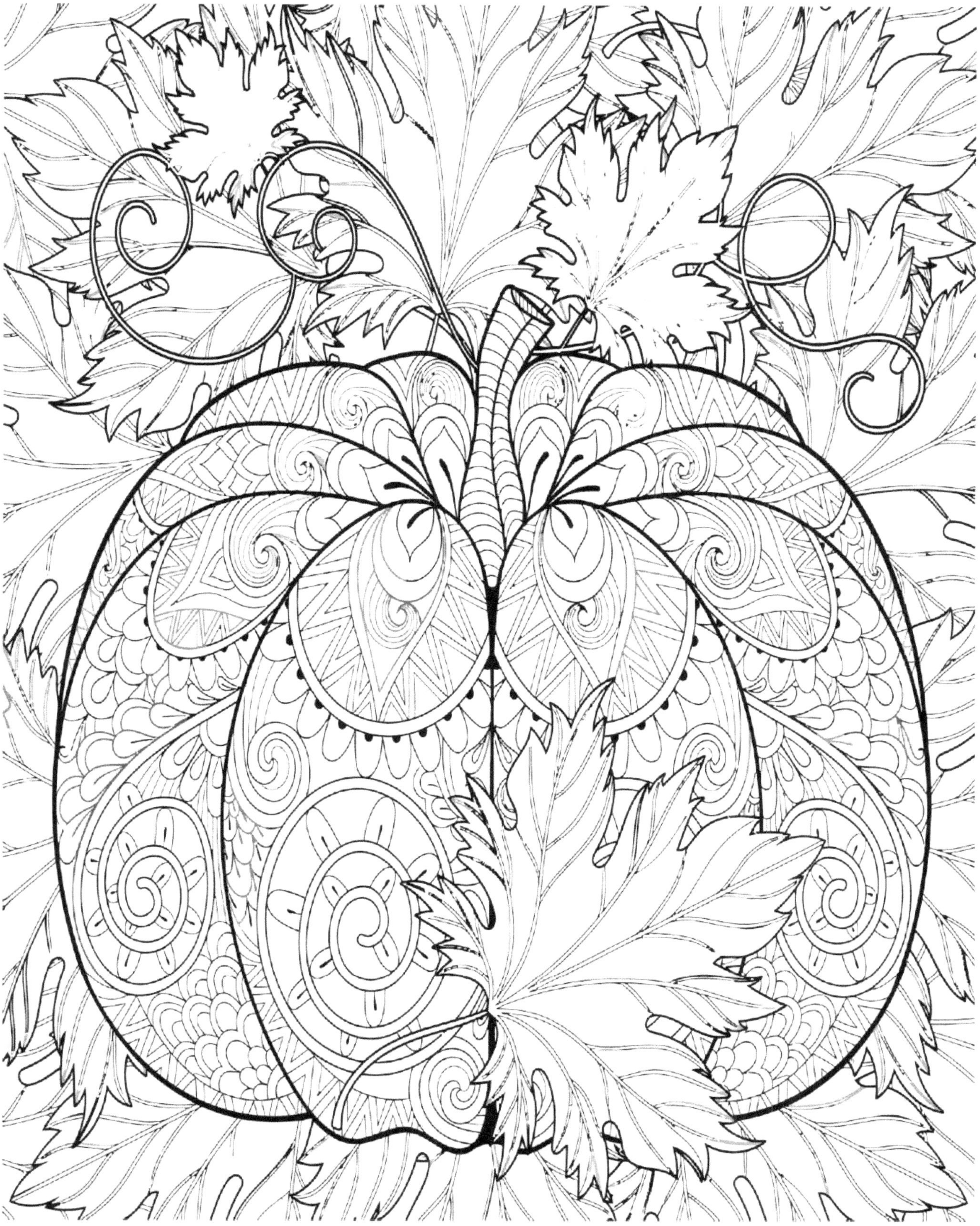

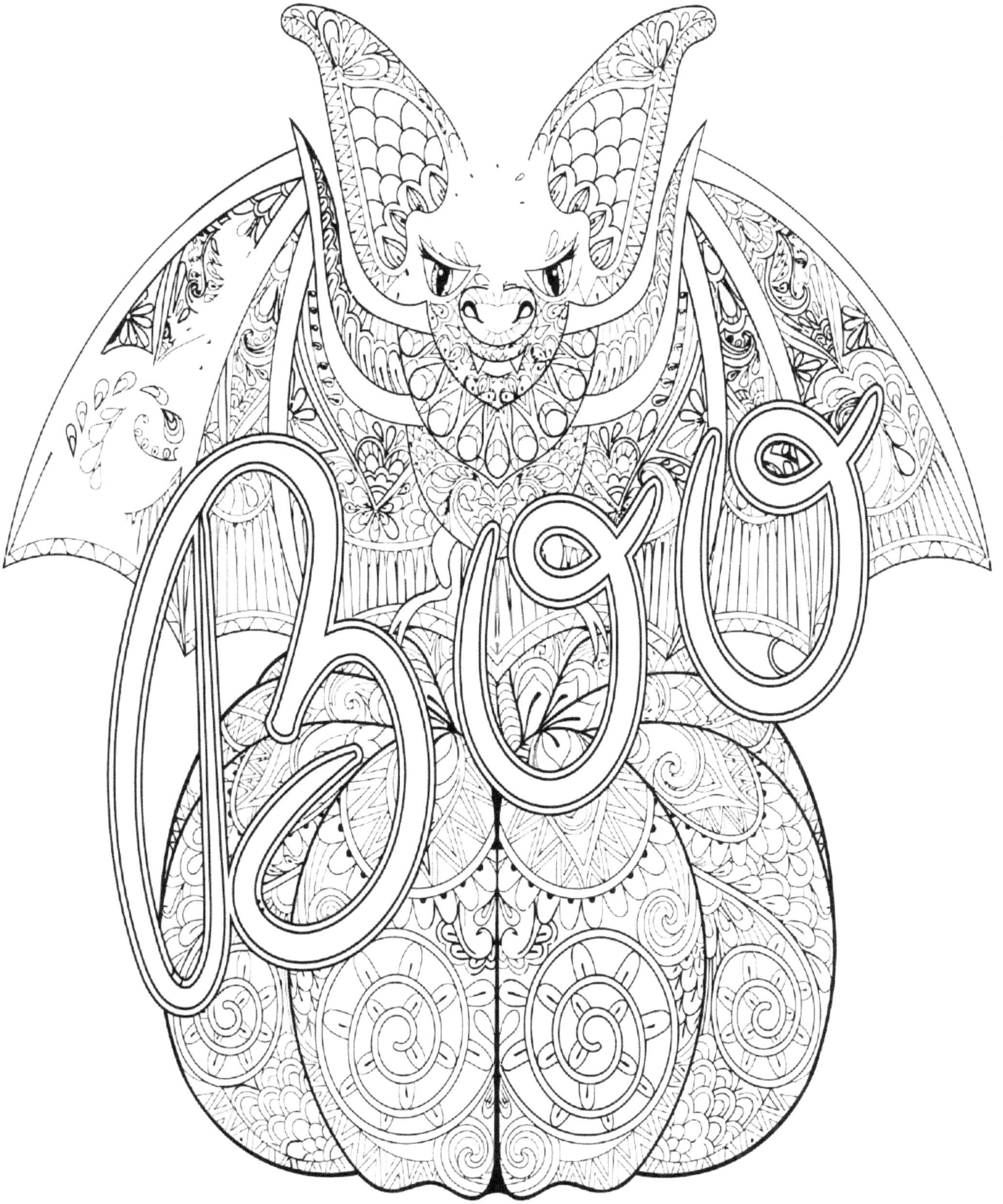
Boo

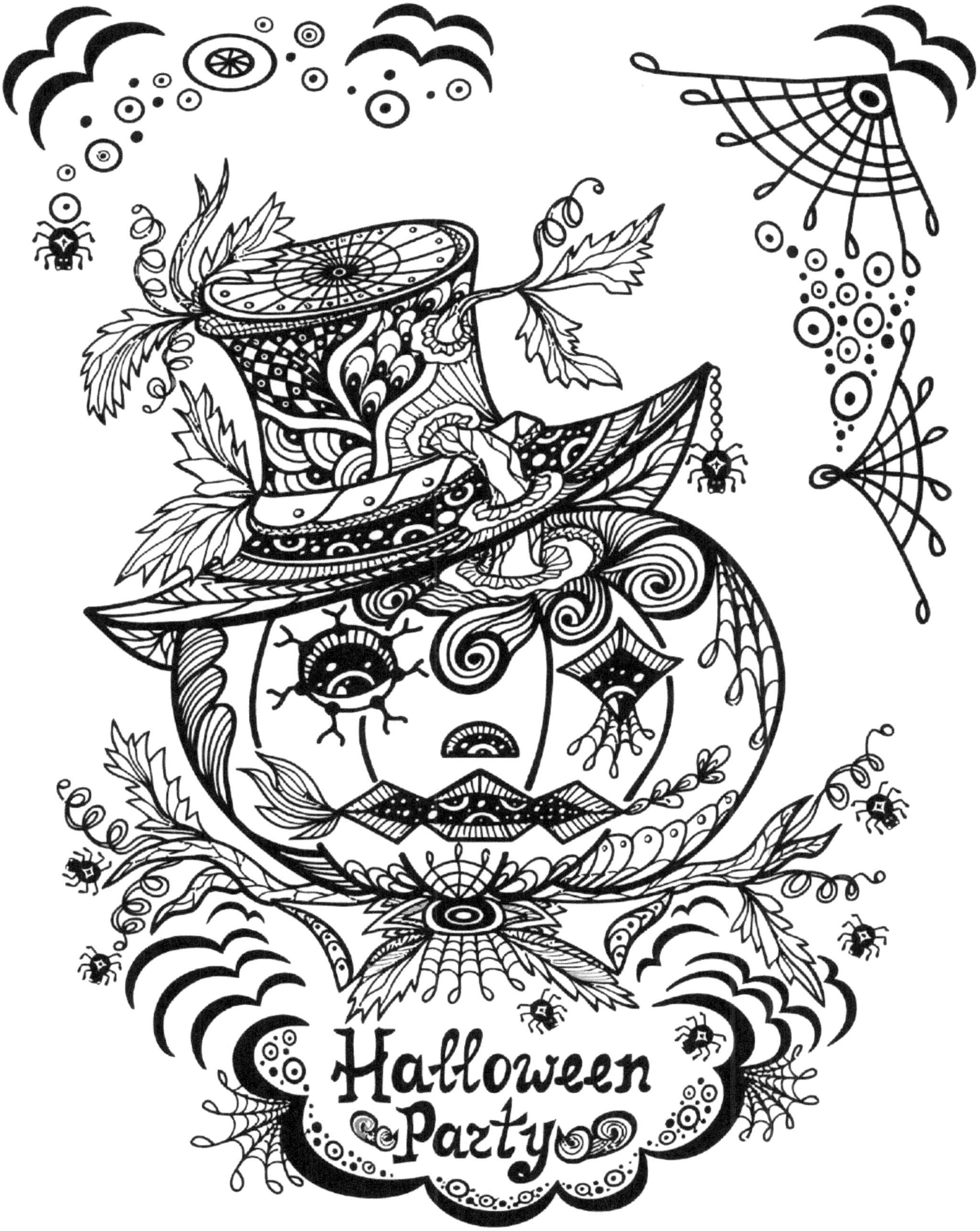
Halloween
Party

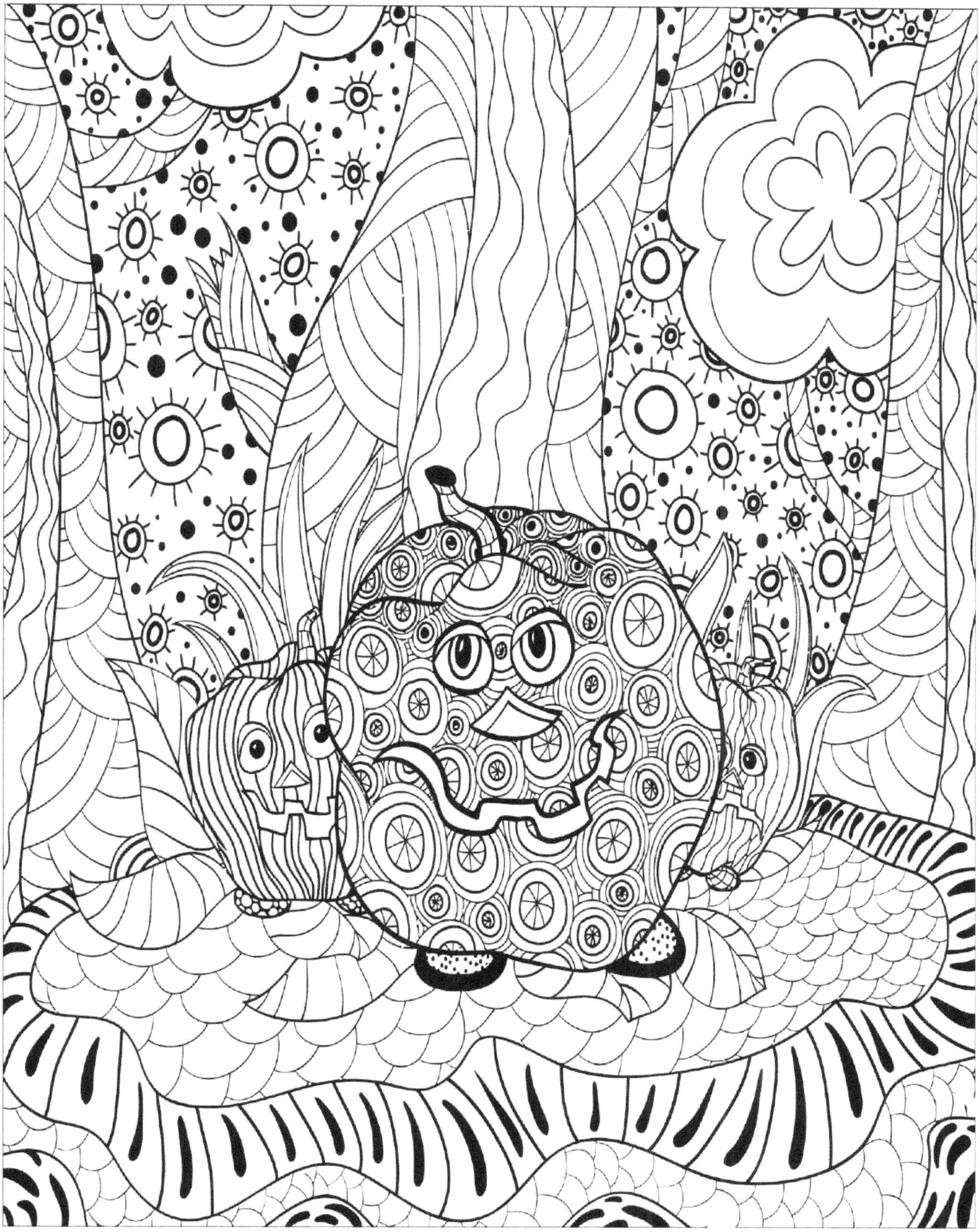

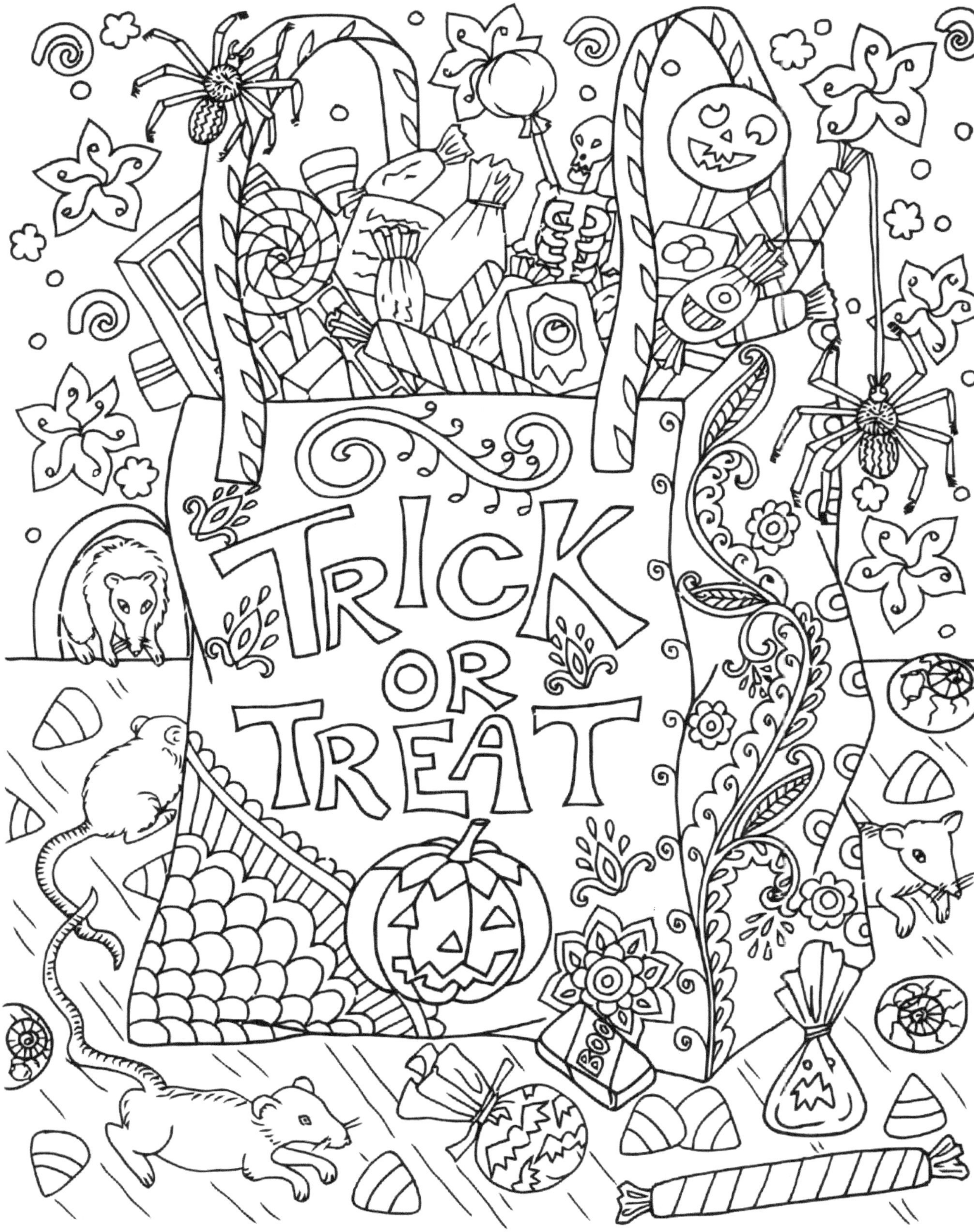
TRICK
OR
TREAT
BOO

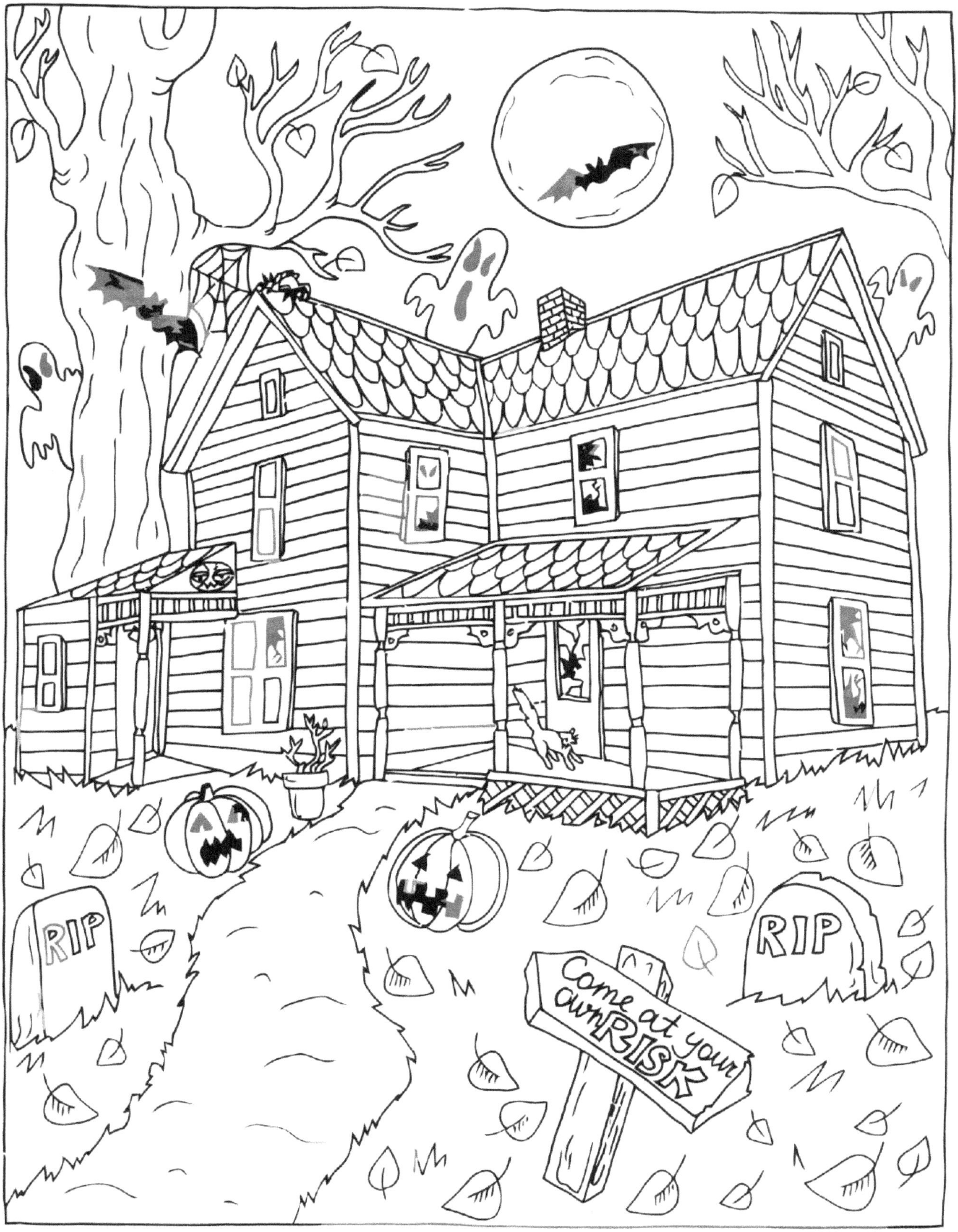
RIP
RIP
Come at your own RISK

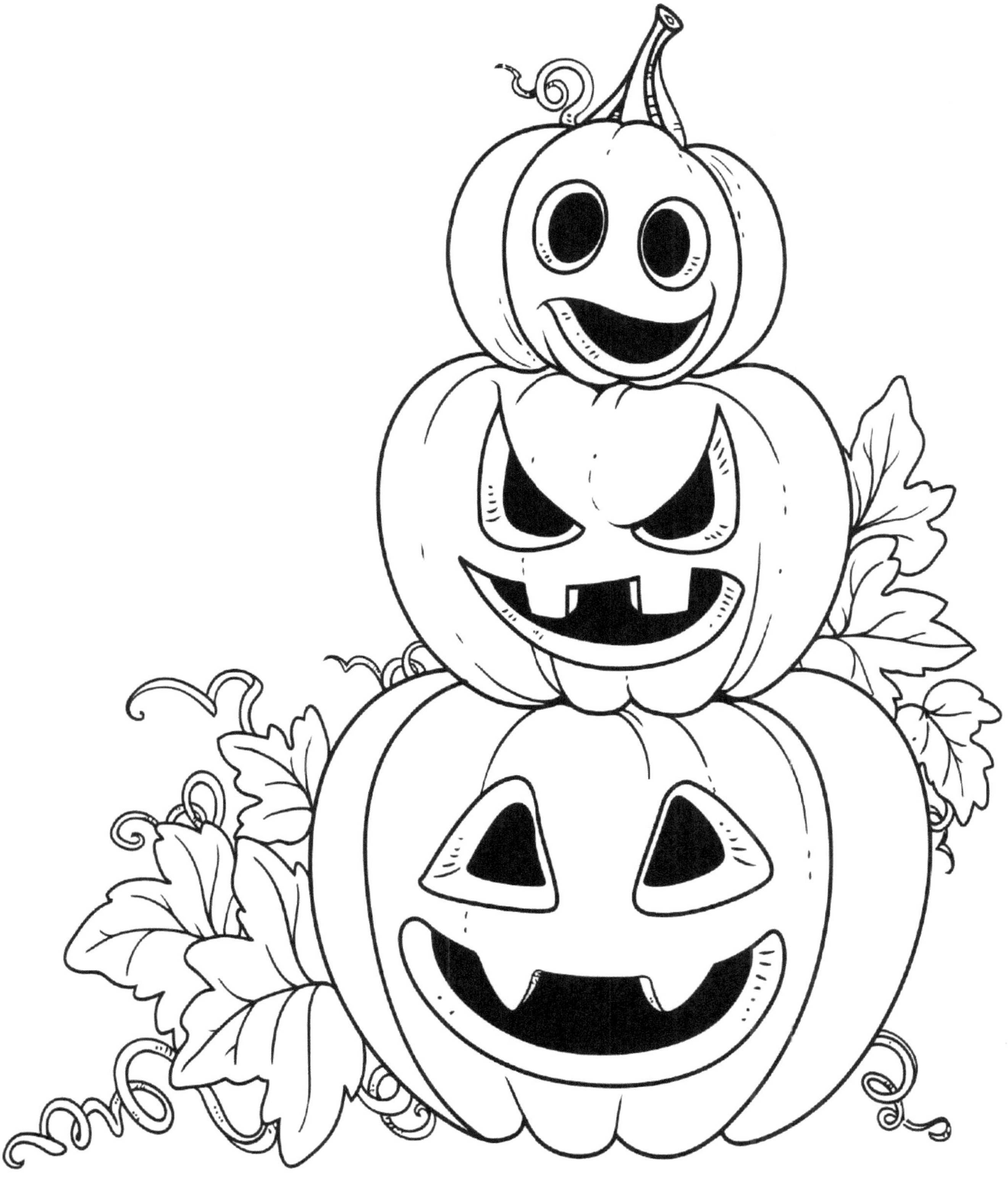

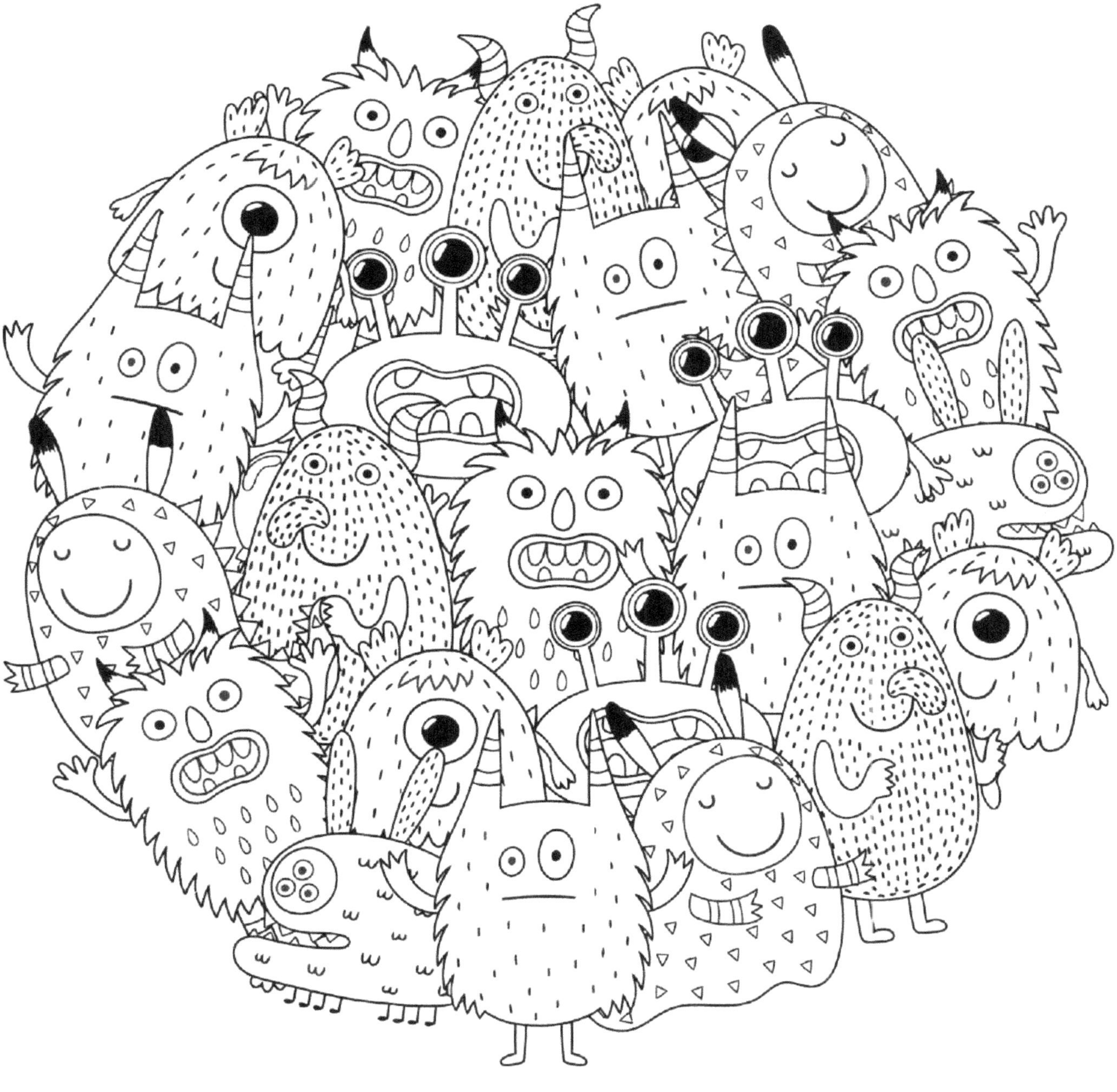

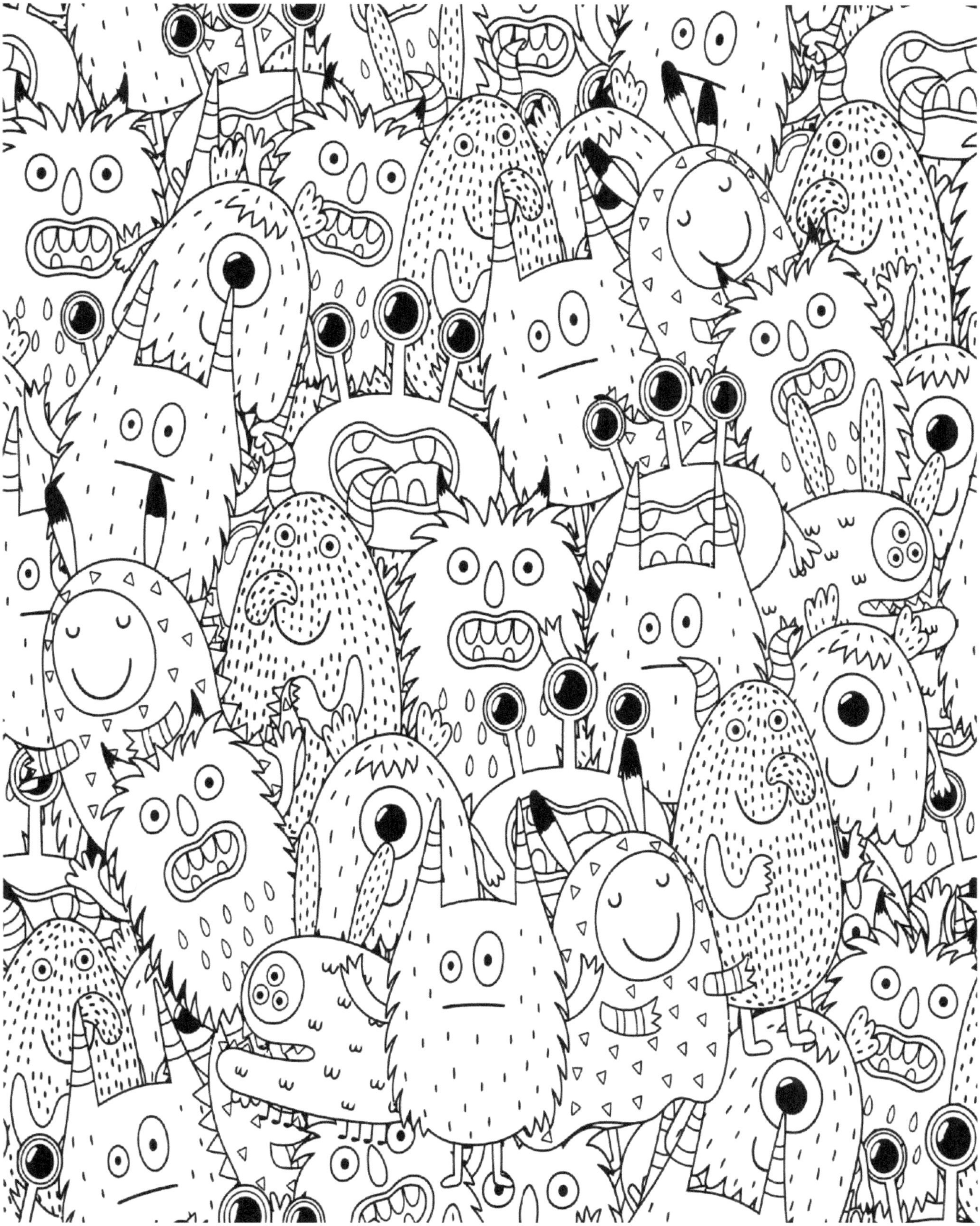

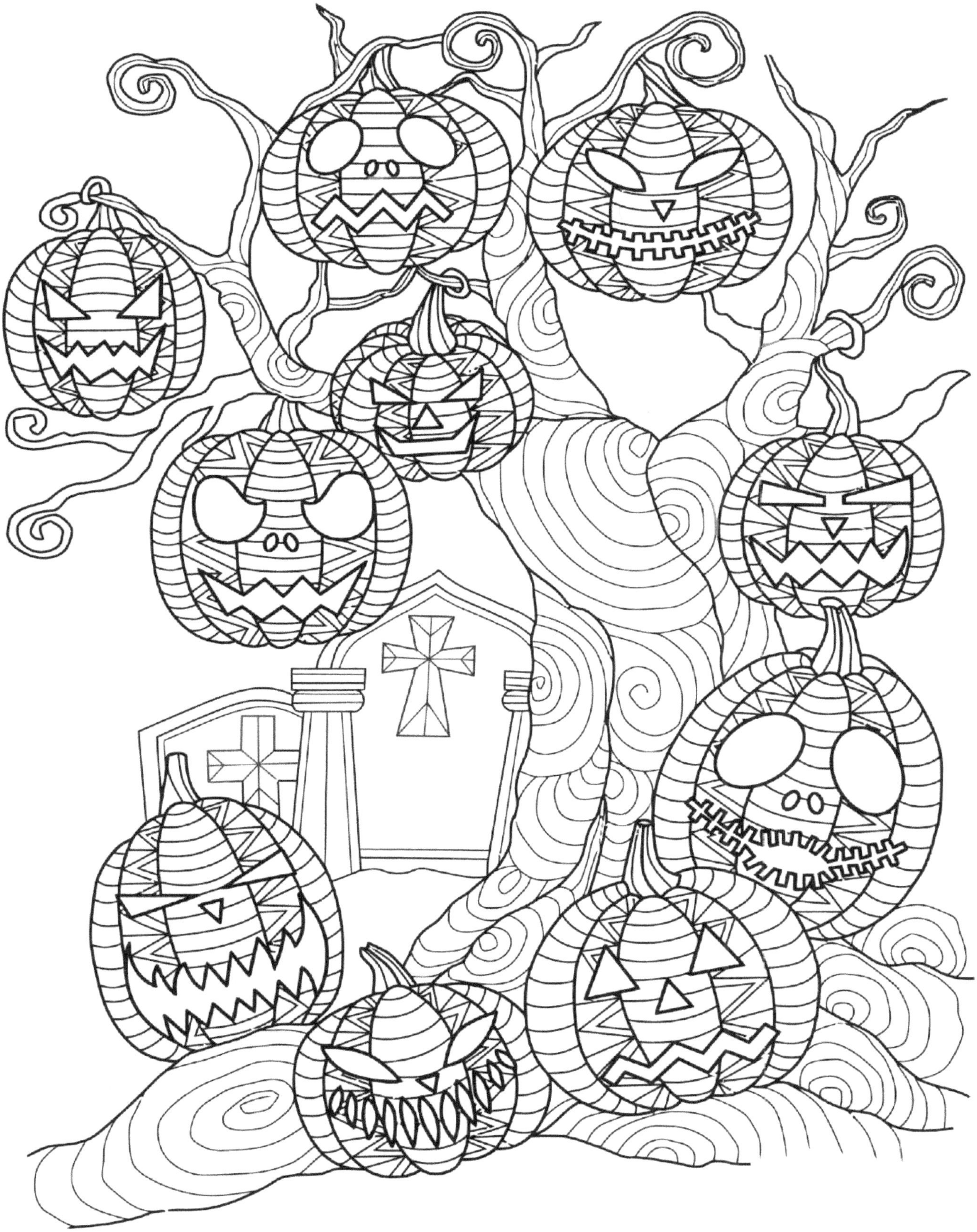

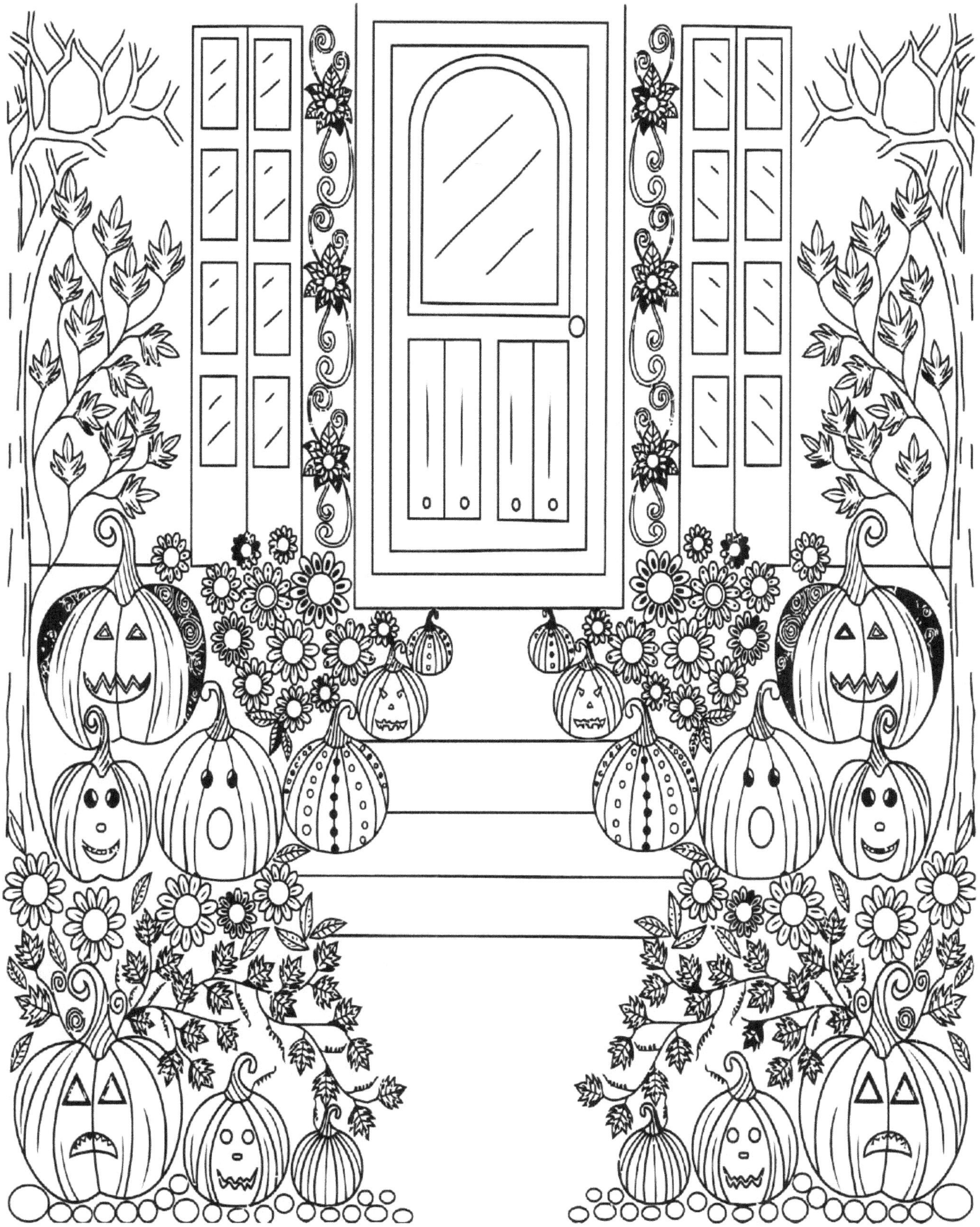

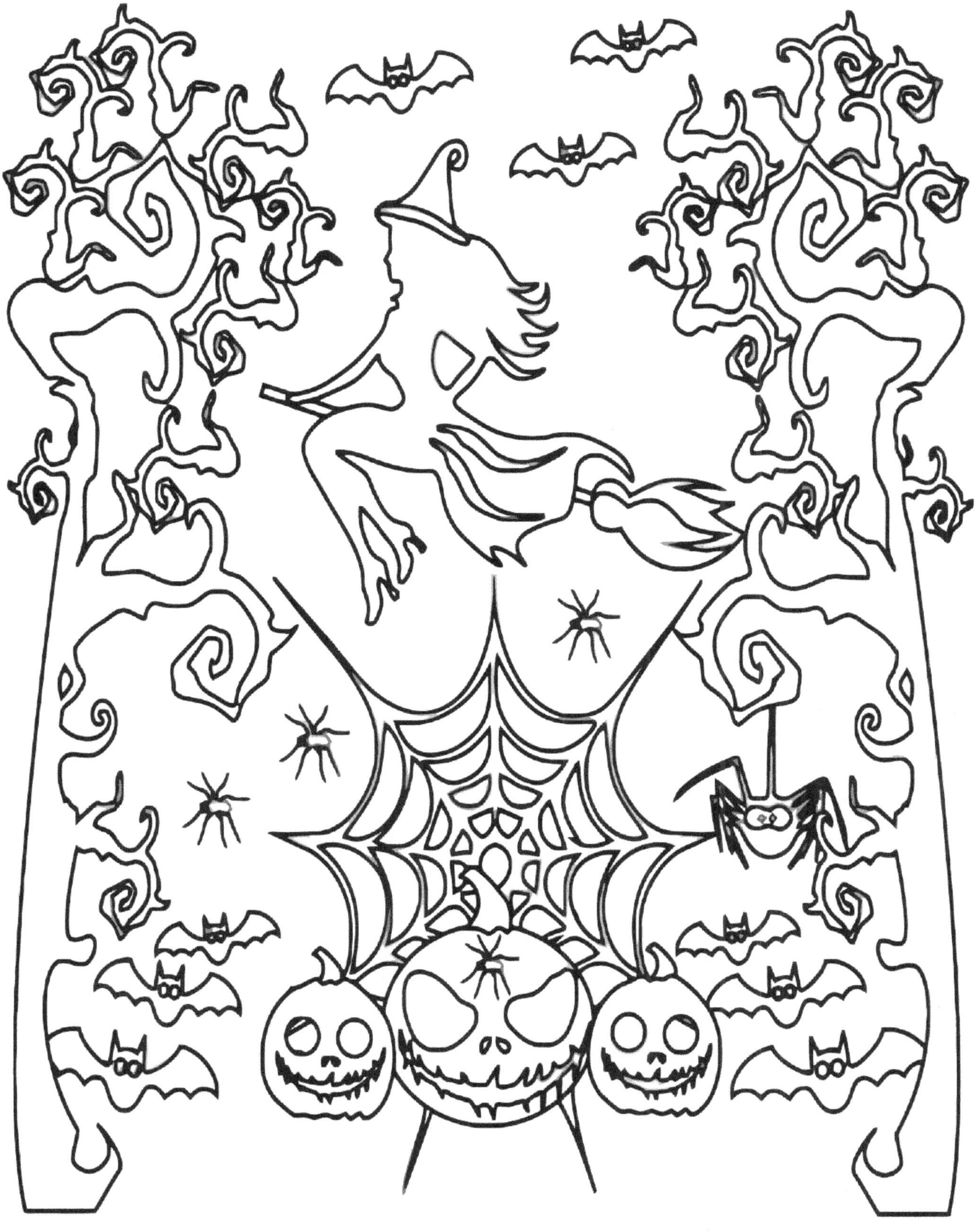

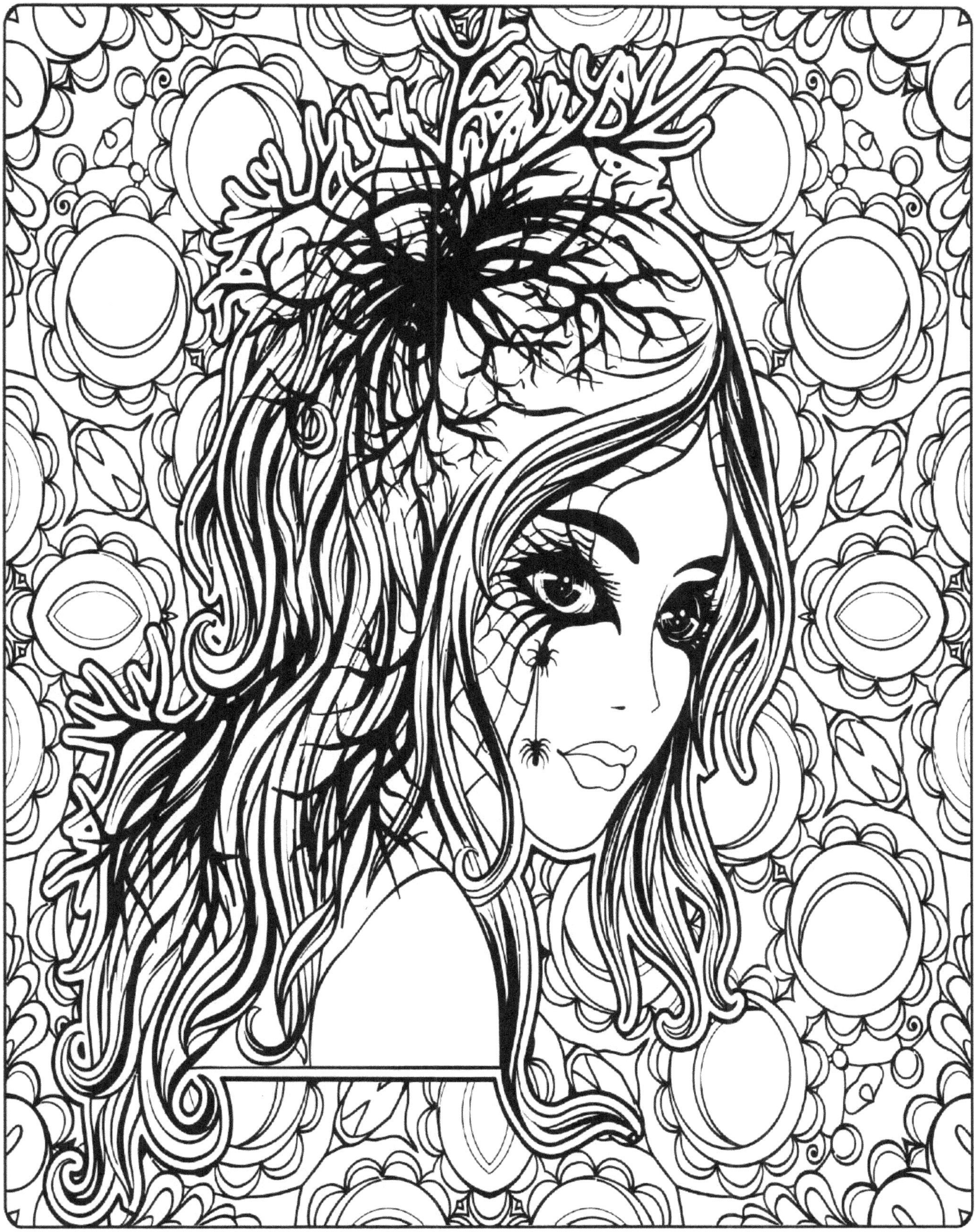

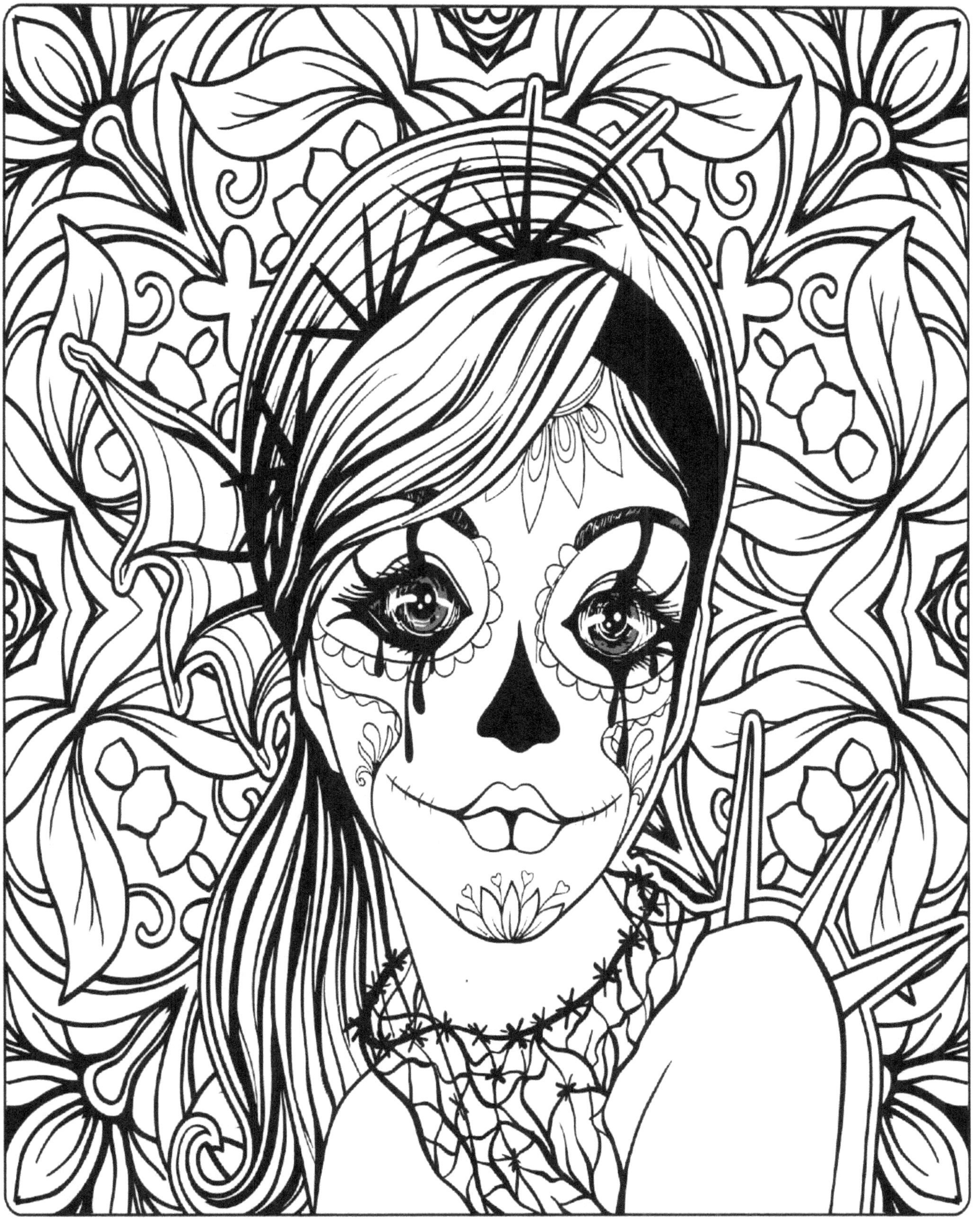

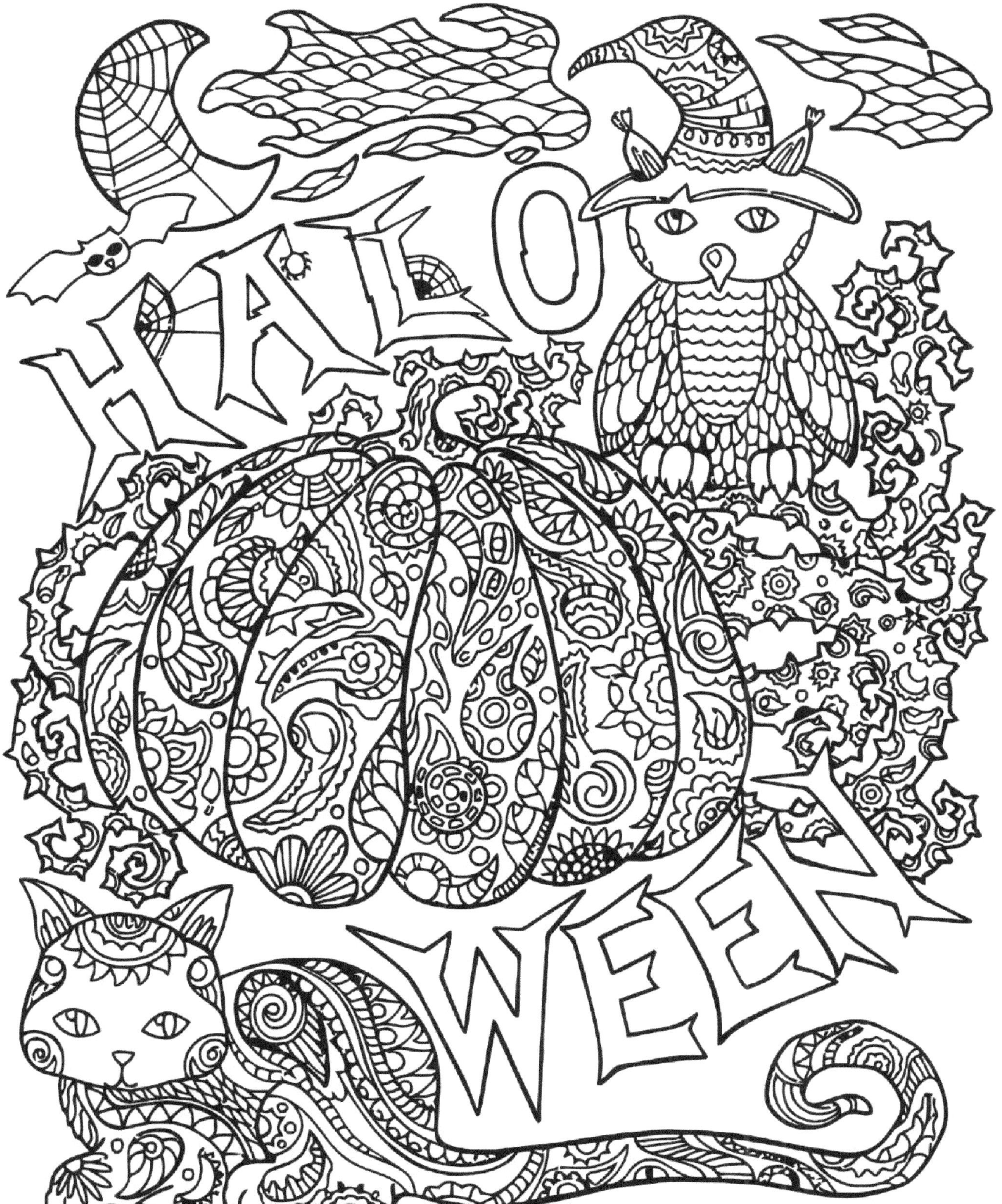
HALLO
WEEN

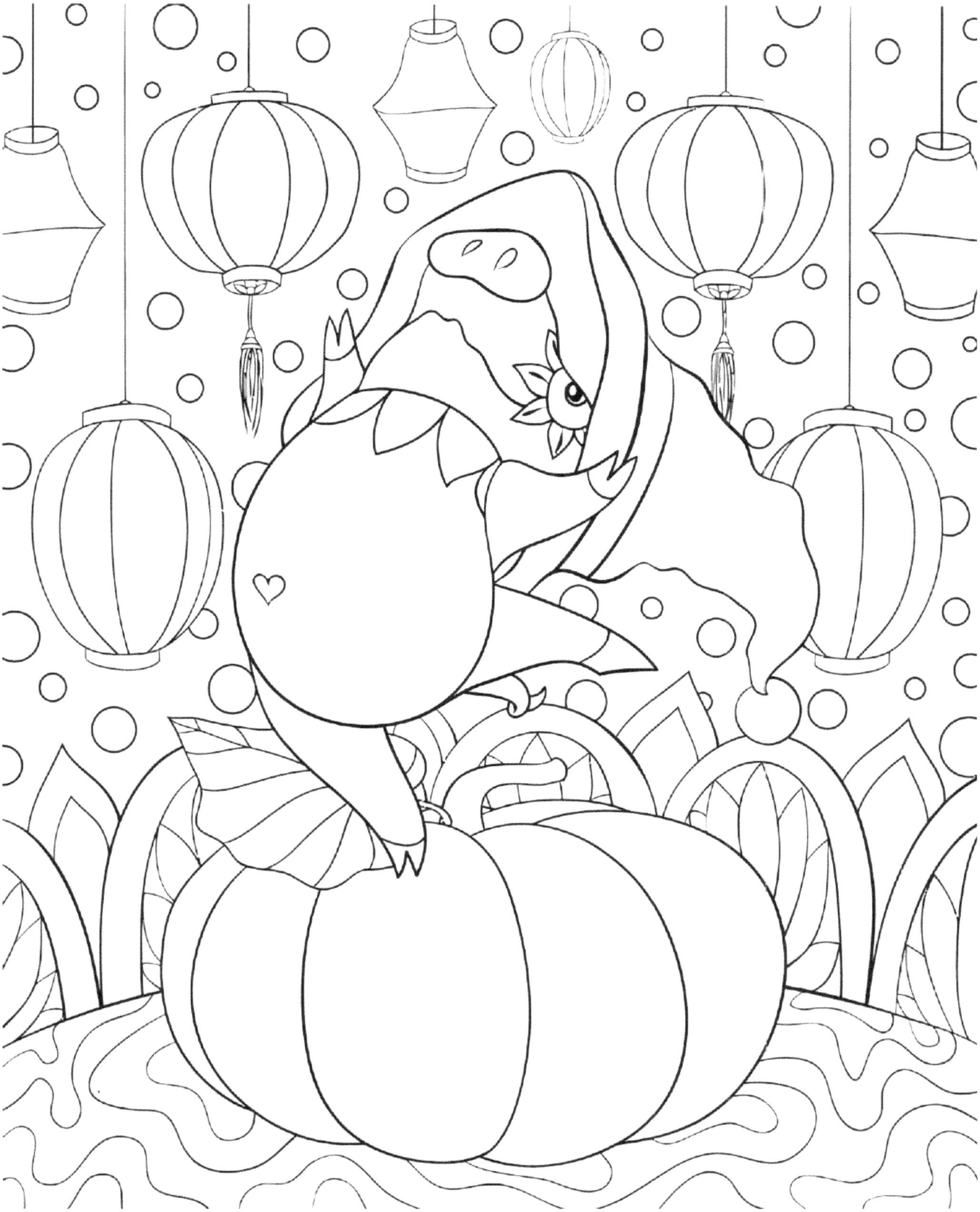

www.ingramcontent.com/pod-product-compliance
Lightning Source LLC
Chambersburg PA
CBHW082115220526
45472CB00009B/2180
* 9 7 9 8 4 5 7 5 3 1 5 6 7 *